REMEMBRANCE, REUNION AND REVIVAL: CELEBRATING A DECADE OF APPALACHIAN STUDIES

*Proceedings Of The
Tenth Annual
Appalachian Studies Conference*

Edited By
HELEN ROSEBERRY

Managing Editor
JANE SHOOK

The Appalachian Consortium was a non-profit educational organization composed of institutions and agencies located in Southern Appalachia. From 1973 to 2004, its members published pioneering works in Appalachian studies documenting the history and cultural heritage of the region. The Appalachian Consortium Press was the first publisher devoted solely to the region and many of the works it published remain seminal in the field to this day.

With funding from the Andrew W. Mellon Foundation and the National Endowment for the Humanities through the Humanities Open Book Program, Appalachian State University has published new paperback and open access digital editions of works from the Appalachian Consortium Press.

www.collections.library.appstate.edu/appconsortiumbooks

This work is licensed under a Creative Commons BY-NC-ND license. To view a copy of the license, visit http://creativecommons.org/licenses.

Original copyright © 1988 by the Appalachian Consortium Press.

ISBN (pbk.: alk. Paper): 978-1-4696-3668-9
ISBN (ebook): 978-1-4696-3670-2

Distributed by the University of North Carolina Press
www.uncpress.org

Table of Contents

INTRODUCTION, *Helen Roseberry* 1

I. APPALACHIAN WOMEN AUTHORS
Interviews With Harriette Arnow:
Looking Beyond The Dollmaker, *Sandra L. Ballard* 3

II. EVALUATING APPALACHIAN STUDIES
Regionalism and Revitalization: Towards a Comparative
Perspective on Appalachian Studies, *Richard Blaustein* 14

The "Brier Sermon" Signpost in Appalachian Studies,
Ricky Cox 21

Appalachian Educational Research in the National Context:
Where We Have Been and Where We Are Going,
Alan J. DeYoung 29

III. PARTNERING FOR RESEARCH
Partnering with the Indigenous: Teaming with the Marshall
Family to Study Old Regular Baptists, *Howard Dorgan* 50

IV. REEVALUATING WOMEN'S ROLES
From: "Fotched-on" Women to the New Feminism:
A Review of Women in Social Service Delivery for Women
in Appalachia, *Karen Tice and* Albie Pabon. 57

V. POETRY READING
Yearning Toward Home and Its Traditions,
Bennie Lee Sinclair 68

VI. UNIVERSALITY IN LITERATURE
R'lyeh in Appalachia: Lovecraft's
Influence on Fred Chappell's Dagon, *Amy Tipton Gray* 73

VII. ECONOMIC DEVELOPMENT AND REDEVELOPMENT
The Rayon Mills in Elizabethton, Tennessee: A Case Study of
Appalachian Economic Development, 1926-1970,
Marie Tedesco 80

VIII. INSTRUCTION AND PROFESSIONAL DEVELOPMENT
Process Instruction in Appalachian Studies - A Case Example
Using Education in Appalachia's Central Highlands,
Mark F. Sohn 91

Chapels in the Mountains, *Marc Sherrod* 95

IX. COVERLET WEAVING
Origins of the Handicraft Revival in the Southern Mountains,
Curtis Wood and *Joan Greene* 108

X. APPALACHIA: CONTRASTS AND SIMILARITIES
A Look at Regional Patterns in the Southern Highlands,
Paul E. Lovingood, Jr. and *Robert E. Reiman* 115

1987 PROGRAM COMMITTEE
Helen Roseberry, Chair

Doyle Bickers
Barry Buxton
Richard Dillingham
Howard Dorgan

Wilburn Hayden
Roberta Herrin
Parks Lanier
Gerald Roberts

Introduction

Prologizing the Tenth Anniversary of the Appalachian Studies Conference, appropriately titled, "Remembrance, Reunion and Revival: Celebrating A Decade of Appalachian Studies," Dr. Carl Ross, who had chaired the previous Conference program, stated in his Introduction in its Proceedings, "The Appalachian Studies Association was formed in 1977 by scholars, teachers, and regional activists who believed that a shared community of ideas and interests had been and would continue to be important for those writing, researching and teaching about things Appalachian."

As he edited those Proceedings, Ross could not have realized that he would be making those same remarks just a few months later to kick-off the 1987 Conference. Even as he drove onto the East Tennessee State University campus the afternoon of March 27, 1987 to register for the Conference, he could not have realized the timeliness of those remarks written just months before, to the evening ahead.

"The first Appalachian Studies Conference was held at Berea, Kentucky in March of 1978." Ross found himself delivering an impromptu keynote address to nearly three-hundred Conference registrants during its 1987 opening night banquet, reminding them that prior to the organization of the Association, "...much of the attention and much of the effort to change came from outside the region." His perspicuous and adroit remarks, prompted by a last-minute cancellation by the scheduled speaker, were delivered in the true essence of the theme.

"The Association was organized to bring together scholars and citizens within the region. I think we more fully realize how dynamic Appalachian society has always been," Ross continued, reflecting on "...a simpler past when neighbors cared for each other."

With an energy reminiscent of that of the First Conference, Ross, appropriately enough during a year in which we had chosen to look back, stepped from behind the podium and concluded, "We are all in it together. If we work together and try to understand each other and each other's goals, maybe we will be the better for it."

Carl Ross received a standing ovation. For he had set the tone for the 1987 Conference.

The warm, sunny weather was remindful of the First Conference, and many of those who had met together that first time and actively worked to shape the format of the Conference as we know it now, had come to reminisce, to share fresh ideas, to listen.

Like the First Conference, this Conference brought forth explorations of a variety of issues, and included, as Sam Gray so aptly stated in his introduction in the 1985 Proceedings, "...certain ideas, issues and positions that were to become the durable content of each annual Appalachian Studies Conference."

The tone of the 1987 Conference is reflected in the papers included in this publication. They are exponents of both the quality and diversity of the Conference. Editorial and budgetary constraints dictated the inclusion of only a representative sampling of those presented.

Through the first decade of its existence the Appalachian Studies Conference managed to accomplish the goals set forth at its initial meeting in Berea, Kentucky in 1978. As the second decade begins, those goals will function as any good foundation will. And as Carl Ross stated, "...maybe we will be the better for it.

> Helen Roseberry, Chair
> 1987 Program Committee"

APPALACHIAN WOMEN AUTHORS
Convenor: Grace Edwards, Radford University
Interviews With Harriette Arnow: Looking Beyond The Dollmaker
Sandra L. Ballard, University of Tennessee
Harriette Arnow's Assessment of Appalachia's Role In America's Industrial Development
Ted Couillard, Georgia Southwestern College
Marjorie Kinnan Rawlings: A Mountain Passage
Louis D. Silveri, Assumption College
What Is The Place of Mary Noailles Murfree Today?
Allison R. Ensor, University of Tennessee

Interviews With Harriette Simpson Arnow: Looking Beyond The Dollmaker

by
Sandra L. Ballard

Harriette Simpson Arnow is much more than the author of a single novel, though most of us think of *The Dollmaker* when we think of her, especially since the 1984 ABC television film with Jane Fonda. When Arnow commented on the film version of her novel, she said worse films have been made of "many greater books" ("Writing and Region").

The Dollmaker was an award-winning novel in 1954. *Saturday Review's* national critics' poll voted it the best novel of the year, and also in 1954, Arnow's story of Gertie Nevels' family was runner-up to Faulkner's *A Fable* for the National Book Award. In 1971, Joyce Carol Oates acknowledged *The Dollmaker* as "our most unpretentious American masterpiece" (2).

But as the title of my presentation suggests, we can learn much about Arnow by looking beyond *The Dollmaker*, as worthy as it is of attention. We should look at her writings before and after *The Dollmaker* to understand the scope of her work. Harriette Arnow wrote other novels as well as non-fiction "social histories," short stories, and essays which have appeared in such publications as *Southern Review, Esquire, Atlantic Monthly, Saturday Review,* and *The Nation*.

When I first met Harriette Arnow in June of 1985 in Morehead, Kentucky, I was fortunate enough to have a brief interview with her after her address to the Appalachian Writers' Association. Since then, in the course of my research on Arnow, I have discovered a number of articles based on interviews that reveal a fascinating picture of the writer who worried that people were trying to ride her to fame "on Jane Fonda's coattails" (Williams B5). When people asked her when she wrote "the Book," meaning *The Dollmaker*, she liked to ask, "which book?" Arnow wanted people to know that she had written more than one novel. It is the purpose of this presentation to inform you or remind you of her other work as a short story writer, novelist, social historian, and essayist, as well as to share some first-hand observations and anecdotes reported by those who interviewed her. Such information should give texture and dimension to your image of Harriette Simpson Arnow as a writer.

When I met Harriette Arnow in June of 1985 at Morehead, I also met John Flynn and his wife Carole Thompson, Arnow's friends from Detroit who had driven her to Morehead for the weekend. John Flynn, a newspaper reporter, was a friend of both the Arnows; Harriette Arnow's husband, Harold, had also been a reporter, and he usually traveled with her, but I learned that evening that Harold Arnow had died of a stroke in February of 1985. From Flynn and Thompson, I learned much of what I'm sharing with you this morning. John Flynn has since written a manuscript about that trip with Harriette Arnow, and he sent me a copy, though it remains unpublished.

Besides answering many of my questions, after Arnow's talk, Flynn asked her if Toney Frazier and I could accompany them back to her room. She agreed, though reluctantly because, as she said to John Flynn in a loud aside, "we can't have a drink in the room with these young people around." When she had been assured that it would be all right, she answered my questions about *The Dollmaker* and other literature over a glass of Old Grandad.

When I told her I had begun working on a book about her, she looked straight at me with her penetrating blue eyes and wanted to know why. She said that I should study "something else, like *Ulysses*, not the Greek one," she said, "the one by that Irish fella." I should write something to help her understand that book. When I protested that there were many books about Joyce but only one about her and I didn't think that one did her justice, she stopped and smiled. She knew the Twayne series book I meant, and she agreed with me. She was obviously tired, so after a while we got up to leave. She repeated that she didn't know why anyone would want to write about her; she encouraged me to write something of my own.

As Arnow told many who asked how she got started as a writer, she did a daring thing in 1934. She left teaching, a career her mother had insisted on, and moved to Cincinnati. She said "it was a short move from Louisville to Cincinnati, but a long, long one in my life" (Address to Appalachian Writers Association). She made up her mind to write and to read the great English and European novels she had missed. She said, "I'd only stop when I had to take some kind of odd job to pay for rent and of course, paper, typewriter ribbons, and postage" (Address to AWA). Her family was scandalized when she moved—a young single woman moving to a big city, living alone, writing. She took a furnished room near the Cincinnati Public Library.

Even though it was the Depression, she was "young and quick," she said, and "could always get a job at something" (Hudson). She said the best-paying job was waitressing "in a good place with tips," a place with short hours and "plenty of busboys" so there was no heavy lifting (Hudson). She also worked as a typist, as a cashier, and as a clerk in the book department of a department store, but she preferred being a waitress because that job left more time for writing (Hudson).

She described that period of her life as "a great time," when "more fiction was being published than non-fiction" though "the reverse is true today," she noted (Address to AWA). She went to the library to read reviews in the *New York Times* and other papers because she "couldn't afford the book page or anything." She remembered that "many of the reviews were given over to what was called 'the proletarian writing,'" which was "usually highly praised." With the help of dictionaries, she learned about "the proletariate" and, she said, "I thought of the poor I had met in the hills and I couldn't consider them as members of the proletariate, proletarians; they were all individuals to me, as were characters in my imagination" (Address to AWA). And certainly that view is responsible in large part for Arnow's reputation as a fiction writer— she does create memorable characters who are individuals.

More than one interviewer observed that listening to Harriette Arnow talk about her characters was like being invited into an imaginary world where the characters were her neighbors. In fact, she admitted that sometimes she knew them "better than anyone, even Harold" and that people in her head were "more alive" than people she knew (Kotlowitz 22).

When asked which writers influenced her, she said that she read Tolstoy, Dostoyevsky, Sidgrid Undset, Zola, Flaubert, and many others when she first moved to Cincinnati, and that they influenced her in at least one way— "length. I want to put it all in—and my novels are all too long" (Miller 95). She claimed to have been influenced by Thomas Hardy, too, "his use of background," she said, and by Milton's prose (Miller 95). She said she wanted "to be able to write the same kind of sentences Milton used in *Aceopaqitica* and other essays. He begins and gradually rises." They made her think of "a wave when the tide's coming in, and they hit you just like a hard wave." She didn't think she could write "a real Miltonic sentence" (Miller 95). But readers who pay attention to the hard-hitting concluding sentences of her stories and novels can see particular examples which demonstrate this technique in Arnow's own prose.

Harriette Simpson wrote short stories in the 1930s and had several published: one called "Marigolds and Mules," in *Kosmos* in 1934; another titled " A Mess of Pork," in *The New Talent* in 1935. *Kosmos* and *The New Talent* were little literary magazines which, she said, "paid in nothing except the glory you felt of the published story and free copies of the magazine" (Hudson).

In 1936 she sold a story to the prestigious *Southern Review* (1 Winter 1936 522-7), when Robert Penn Warren was its editor: "I was so proud when he accepted this story and paid $25...lt on top of the world" (Hudson). The story was "Washerwoman's Day," which became her most anthologized story. Warren, Purser, and Brooks included it in their textbook anthology *An Approach to Literature* (New York: Appleton-Century-Crofts, 1939, 1952); Brooks and Warren also anthologized it in a collection of stories from the *Southern Review* (*Anthology of Stories from the Southern Review*. Ed. Cleanth Brooks and Robert Penn Warren. Baton Rouge, La.: Louisiana State Univ. Press, 1953). More recently, in 1979, Arnow's story "Fra Lippi and Me" was published in the *Georgia Review* (33(Winter 1979) 867-75), and eighteen unpublished short stories remain in the Arnow Special Collection at the University of Kentucky.

Her short stories led to her trying a longer report, her first novel, *Mountain Path*. She was working on that when she got a letter from Harold Strauss, editor of a New York publishing company called Covici, which also published the work of John Steinbeck. The editor had read one of her stories in a magazine and wanted to know if she had anything longer. She sent him what she had of *Mountain Path*. She said, "It wasn't finished. It was mostly just a collection of characters" (Hudson). But to her surprise, he liked it and told her to get some action in it and make a novel. She remembered, "Oh, I stopped working completely and did nothing but write on that novel" (Hudson). She explained, "I quit my job and took most of my scanty savings and laid in a great deal of condensed milk and oatmeal and bread and did nothing but write until I had what I thought was a novel" (Kotlowitz 22). Arnow said that when the editor told her to put in action, she "put in every kind of action you could: moonshining, murder, romance" (Silberman 3).

She was 28 years old when her first novel was published in 1936. *Mountain Path* is the story of Louisa Sheridan, a young woman who, like Harriette Simpson, had taken a teaching job in backwoods Kentucky because she didn't have the money to continue in school. Though the main character had Harriette Simpson's middle name—Louisa—and though her mother complained, "Everybody will think you fell in love with a moonshiner down here," she explained that the book is not "autobiographical" (Miller 91). Arnow told her friend John Flynn, "Was I on top of the world, except Momma was furious...She wrote and said, "Why don't you write about nice people?'" (Flynn 25).

Fortunately, the critics were more pleased with *Mountain Path* than her mother. Arnow said, "It's a wonder I didn't burst open like the frog in the fable. I was so puffed with pride and glory when I read the reviews, especially the one in the *New York Times*. All the reviews were surprisingly good for the first novel..." (Address to AWA). But she didn't make much money with this novel, "only a few hundred dollars," she told Flynn, because she signed a contract with a clause that limited her royalties. She said, "(*Mountain Path*) sold fairly well, but I was dumb. I didn't have an agent. I made only five cents on some of the copies instead of full royalties" (Flynn 26).

In addition to writing those short stories and her first novel, she also worked for the Federal Writers Project, where she met Harold Arnow in 1938. She told Flynn that when she went to work for Roosevelt's WPA Writer's Project, writing guides to Ohio, Harold was one of her editors. It was, she said, "the first and only time anyone told (her) what to write" (Flynn 27).

She claimed that Harold was more predisposed to marriage than she was: "I was in no humor to get married," she said. "I thought it would be the end of my writing. But he was wild to get married," and Harold wanted "all the things that men want, like a place in the country." But she wished they had found a place with electricity, one closer to town. She said to Flynn, "Why it suddenly hit me that I should marry this man, who seemed to have all the virtues, I do not know" (Flynn 27). It seems she both asked and answered her own question. Years later, their affection for each other was evident. During an interview at home in 1983, when Harold left the house to collect wood for the fireplace, she worried aloud about his arthritis and observed that "managing a husband was nothing like managing a character;" then, when she left the room, Harold Arnow fretted about his wife's chain smoking (Kotlowitz18).

The Arnows married in 1939 and bought a farm on Little Indian Creek on the Big South Fork of the Cumberland River ("Personal Recollections" 14). In a piece called "Personal Recollections," published in *Appalachian Heritage*, she described their farm as a "beautiful place with steep hills for timber and a valley for crops" (14).

The Arnows planned to live there and write and practice subsistence farming. However, she soon realized there was no time for anything except subsistence. She said, "We cooked and heated with coal, used kerosene lights, and water from a hard-water spring" ("Personal Recollections" 14). She "gardened, canned, jellied, preserved, pickled, churned, (and) grew chickens, ... and through it all struggled against soot and coal dust" (14). They called their home there the "Submarginal Manor." She said she did "practically no writing, though *Hunter's Horn* was in (her) head" (14). And she felt particularly frustrated because a publisher, Macmillan, wanted to see a novel manuscript—Covici-Freide, publisher of *Mountain Path*, had gone out of business (14).

The Arnows lived on their farm near Keno, Kentucky, for about five years, from 1939-1944. She said that she "despised the life" but "loved the place and the people." She "not only learned much, but in trying to do what the hill people did with ease," she said, "admiration grew with understanding," and she explained what happened to that place in an essay she wrote for *The Nation* in 1970—an essay entitled "Progress Reached Our Valley" ("Personal Recollections" 14).

However, she did not confide to many about everything that had happened to them while living there on that farm. Flynn says that "seldom did she discuss the death of her babies," though there are two small graves beside her husband's and now her own in Kentucky. She told Flynn that she "was just no good at child bearing," that their first child, a son, was stillborn, and that their third child, a daughter, died a few hours after birth (18).

In between, in 1941, their daughter Marcella had been born healthy, though Arnow often worried about her, especially since they lived in such an isolated place. When Marcella was nearly three years old, she became ill with a high fever and "quivered as though she might go into convulsions" (Flynn 18). Arnow was there alone with her because Harold was at work in Detroit.

She told Flynn, "I carried her (Marcella) up the hill, so muddy I couldn't have gotten her out any other way, and got a ride in a coal truck, which took her to Burnside. There she was doctored" (18). Readers of *The Dollmaker* no doubt recall that unforgettable opening scene in which Gertie Nevels carries her three-year-old child Amos by muleback to the highway, where she stops a car to take them into town to a doctor. But before they can travel to town, Gertie must use her carving knife to open her son's windpipe so that he can breathe. When Flynn asked if there were a connection between Marcella and Amos, between Gertie and herself, Arnow replied, "I couldn't have cut into Marcella's throat... I don't think" (19). But few acquainted with Arnow could doubt that she was as tough as Gertie.

Determined to prevent the recurrence of such an emergency, Arnow said she "stayed in Burnside and made arrangements to rent the upstairs of a home, then went back to the farm and sold the heating stove and the cattle" (Flynn 19). Harold Arnow had hoped to return to the farm and had not been eager to leave in the first place. But "the Government told him to get a job that in some way would help the country." He found a job as a newspaper reporter in Detroit. Arnow remembered that "he came back once, only once, during the year or more" before she took Marcella to Burnside and then went to join him (Flynn 17).

In Detroit, living in wartime housing, she finished writing her second novel, *Hunter's Horn*. She had become one of the immigrants that she would write about in her third novel. By then, her daughter was more than seven, and she also had a two-year-old son, Thomas. She had already published two stories from the novel manuscript. In July of 1942, *Esquire*, had published "The Two Deer Hunters" (74-5, 96). Knowing that *Esquire*, at that time, would not be interested in a story by a woman, she had signed it "H.L. Simpson" and slyly sent along a picture of her brother-in-law. She smiled mischievously when she told Kotlowitz, "It worried me a little, that big lie, but I thought if they wanted a story, let them have it. So I did" (24). It was Harriette Arnow's way of getting back at the male-dominated publishing industry.

The Atlantic Monthly had also published a story from the manuscript of her second novel, a story titled "The Hunter" and signed "H. Arnow." She honored her husband Harold by naming him as the co-author of the piece. Because he could read her handwriting, Harold Arnow willingly assumed, for nearly forty-five years, many of the traditional duties of a writer's spouse; he was his wife's typist, editor, friend, and best listener (Kotlowitz 18). Most who knew Harriette Arnow agreed that without her husband, Harold, much of her writing would have never reached a publisher, for the business of typing, corresponding, and copy-editing took too much time away from her writing. In 1983, Harold Arnow whispered to a reporter that "Harriette doesn't care if she gets the publicity or not, but I like to see her get it" (Kotlowitz 18).

And in 1949 she did receive publicity for *Hunter's Horn*. Her story of a poor Kentucky family and their struggles to survive while the father, Nunnley Ballew, neglects them and his land to pursue relentlessly a red fox called King Devil was a best seller. It was offered as a Fiction Book Club selection and named by the *New York Times Book Review* as one of the year's ten best novels. It also won best novel of the year in 1949 in the *Saturday Review* national critics' poll, in a year when it was competing with Orwell's *1964*.

During several interviews, Arnow revealed that she had taken *Hunter's Horn* through many revisions. She said that she "wrote the beginning of *Hunter's Horn* (the first chapter) 17 or 18 times, that she "was trying to tell too much" ("Ahead of Her Time" 7). She described the writing style she aspired to in this novel as one that was "not wordy, a narrative with no adverbs and few adjectives" (Flynn 45). She explained: "Language, if you use it right, doesn't need an adverb. Like, "He yelled angrily, Get out of here!" If he yelled, of course he was angry" (Flynn 45).

Though she was living in Detroit when she wrote *Hunter's Horn*, she drew on her first-hand knowledge of people she had known in Pulaski County, Kentucky. And in her own opinion, expressed to Flynn and others, in *Hunter's Horn* she had created a richer, more human cast of characters than in *The Dollmaker*. "Some have said it is a better book than *The Dollmaker*. I believe it is," she said (Flynn 42).

Occasionally, she would skirt the question about which was her favorite book by remarking, "it would be like saying one of my children was my favorite child. When I'm writing a book it's my favorite" (Bright & Girard 12). In her old age, however, she had taken to defending *Hunter's Horn* as her best book (Flynn 40-1). Understandably, I think, she was unhappy that the popularity of *The Dollmaker* caused the public to perceive her as a one-book author. But Flynn explained that it was more than that: as a result of various publishing agreements she had entered into, "rights to her books had been tied in knots, preventing *Mountain Path, Hunter's Horn,* and *The Dollmaker* from being printed in trilogy form" (41). She had admired the writings of Conrad Richter, particularly his trilogy (*The Trees, The Fields,* and *The Town*) in which he recorded the pioneer migration across the Allegheny Mountains, as she had written of the migration from the Appalachians to the northern cities (Flynn 41). She did not live to see the University Press of Kentucky untie the tangle of publication agreements so that readers now can have her trilogy as a matched set of books on their shelves, but she would have been pleased.

Flynn claims that "more than the money she never made, more even than the fame that never came her way, she was most aggrieved that the young people who asked her questions about Gertie Nevels, who was from Ballew,

Kentucky, had not been introduced to Nunn Ballew, from *Hunter's Horn*" (41). He reports that "by her own measurement of a great novel—'one where the reader lives with the characters, like *Fathers and Sons'* —*Hunter's Horn* was a greater achievement than her most famous work" (*The Dollmaker*) (Flynn 42).

Even before *The Dollmaker* was so well received in 1954, Arnow had begun work on a non-fiction project, a history book titled *Seedtime on the Cumberland*, which was published in 1960. This non-fiction book, which she had researched for roughly 20 years, reconstructs the transitional years of early exploration and settlement from 1780 to 1803 along the Cumberland River in southern Kentucky and middle Tennessee. Arnow's view of history makes the time and place very real. She explained that "times and places were mingled in (her) head. The past was part of the present, close as the red cedar water bucket in the kitchen... Two things tied all time together ... the land and the Cumberland" ("Foreword" xii). In 1961, Arnow's *Seedtime Comes to the Cumberland* received an award of merit, announced in the *Tennessee Historical Quarterly*, which cited it for "meticulous documentation, painstaking research, and colorful writing" (299). Also in 1961, Arnow won recognition from the *Tenessee Historical Quarterly* for her article "The Pioneer Farmer and His Crops in the Cumberland Region;" she was awarded the Moore Memorial Award for the best article of 1960 in the *Quarterly*. When a storyteller as talented as Harriette Simpson Arnow turns to history, history comes alive.

Three years later, in 1963, Harriette Arnow's second non-fiction book, *Flowering of the Cumberland*, was published. She explained that it covered the same time period, so it was not a "sequel," but rather "a companion piece" ("Introduction" xi). Having already written of the pioneer as an individual, a lonely explorer or solitary settler, she turned next in *Flowering of the Cumberland* to "the pioneer as a member of society" (xi). Her prose in these works is often as captivating as in her fiction.

In 1977, she wrote a third non-fiction book, *Old Burnside*. It is partly a history of her hometown of Burnside, Kentucky, and partly a personal reminiscence of her family and her growing up, written for the Kentucky Bicentennial Bookshelf. She complained that what started out as a history turned out, at the insistence of her editors, to be a more personal, biographical work than she had planned. She said it turned out to be "one of those awful I, I, I books."

When she talked about her next novel, *The Weedkiller's Daughter*, published in 1970, Arnow acknowledged that it had not been a critical or a popular success, though she reported that she got letters from readers who told her it was the best book she had ever written. This novel, set in a Detroit suburb in the mid-1960s, focuses on the Schnitzer family: a father obsessed with killing weeds and destroying nature; his cold superficial wife; his militant young son; and his daughter, Susie, a rebellious teenager with a social conscience.

Though Gertie Nevels makes an appearance as a character called "the Primitive," Arnow explained she had abandoned Kentucky materials when she resumed fiction writing at least partly because she had never wanted to be labeled as a writer who had concerns exclusively with one area or ideology. She said, "I don't like to be labeled, but there's nothing I can do about it" ("Ahead of Her Time" 7). She could rattle off a list of "labels" with which she had been tagged: a realist, a naturalist, an Appalachian writer, a regionalist, feminist, Marxist, even a transcendentalist writer. Arnow preferred to be called simply "a writer," she said. She pointed out that *Hunter's Horn* and *The Dollmaker* had both been translated in many languages, so they must have more than regional appeal ("Ahead of Her Time" 7). She chose to address a different set of problems in her fiction to make it harder to be "pigeonholed."

Arnow and her husband had moved to a 40-acre farm outside of Ann Arbor, Michigan after the war, around 1949. They didn't like the idea of living in "suburbia," like the Schnitzers in her novel; they said they lived in "exurbia." One interviewer who visited them there described the inside, where books lined the walls of every room except the kitchen, "where magazines from *Connoisseur* to *The Nation* were strewn on the living room coffee table, where stacks of newspapers were "piled high against one wall." The Arnows had nicknamed their place "Bedlam" (Kotlowitz 15).

Kotlowitz described Arnow's study as a small room where all the furniture is built to her size, small, like a miniature dollhouse. "When she (wrote), she (sat) on a child's wooden chair which (was) no more than a foot off the ground, her spiral notebook cradled on her knees. When she (typed), ... she (sat) on an antiquated wooden milk crate turned on its side." The room has a hanging light and a raw concrete floor, and she said it reminded her of "a gangster's den." But she liked it. She explained how she drew the curtains so no one could see in and turned her hearing aid off so she couldn't hear anyone knocking. That way, nothing disturbed her when she was trying to write (Kotlowitz 15).

In 1983, she admitted that she was working on another book, though she only called it "a long manuscript," and when asked what it was about, she usually said "it's about people." But when she was at the University of Tennessee in 1984, she went a bit further to say "it is set in 1861 and '62, in the same south central part of Kentucky" as some of her other writing. She explained, "Kentucky is part of the Union, and Tennessee is part of the Confederacy," but she said she didn't dwell much on battles ("Writing and Region"). She told John Flynn before she died that she had completed over seven hundred pages of this manuscript and that it needed to be revised.

So then, for her last two novels, one published in 1974, entitled *The Kentucky Trace: A Novel of the American Revolution*, and the other as yet unpublished, but about the American Civil War, Harriette Arnow had turned back to her knowledge of Kentucky and United States history. Certainly she was disappointed in the unenthusiastic response *Kentucky Trace* received, though she hardly ever mentioned the novel in interviews. She said that Kentucky had never reviewed many of her books and that she had fewer letters from readers in Kentucky than from any other state. Even though she received the state's highest award for the arts, the Milner Award, in 1983, and was honored by Berea with an outstanding alumni award that same year, the attention came, she thought, because of the Fonda film. She said, "It kind of hurts" (Kotlowitz 18).

Arnow went to Kentucky annually to visit family and friends and to teach at Hindman Settlement School. It was at Hindman that she fell sick with pneumonia in 1985. She was taken to the University of Kentucky hospital where she felt "incarcerated, imprisoned" with a nurse who hated her: the nurse had taken her cigarettes. Soon she was well enough to transfer to the University of Michigan hospital and then home, where a nurse and a housekeeper came by daily. On March 22, 1986 she died in her sleep. She had once said that when she died, she wanted her ashes scattered on the grave of Ronald Reagan, but that, sad to say, he'd probably outlive her (Flynn). On May 16, 1986, her ashes were buried at Keno, Kentucky.

But her writing, of course, has a life of its own. The writer whose imagination and talent gave us *The Dollmaker*, also gave us four other novels—*Mountain Path, Hunter's Horn, Weedkiller's Daughter,* and *Kentucky Trace*.

WORKS CITED

"Ahead of Her Time."*The Berea Alumnus*, July-August 1983, 5-7.

Arnow, Harriette Simpson. Address to Appalachian Writers Association. Lecture given at Morehead State University at Morehead, Kentucky, 29 June 1985

__ "Fra Lippi and Me."*Georgia Review*, 33 (Winter 1979), 867-75.

__ "The Hunter." *Atlantic Monthly*, 174 (Nov.1944), 79-84.

__ (published as Harriette L. Simpson) "Marigolds and Mules." *Kosmos*, 3 (August-Sept. 1934), 3

__ (published as Harriette Simpson). "A Mess of Pork. "*The New Talent*, 1 (Oct.-Dec. 1935, 4-11.

__ "Personal Recollections. "*Appalachian Heritage*, 1 (Fall 1973), 11-15.

__ "The Pioneer Farmer and His Crops in the Cumberland Region." *Tennessee Historical Quarterly*, 19:4 (Dec. 1960), 291-327.

__ "Progress Reached Our Valley." 211 (28 Dec. 1970), 684-7.

(published under H.L. Simpson). "The Two Hunters." *Esquire*, 18 (July 1941), 74-5, 96.
(published as Harriette L. Simpson). "Washerwoman's Day." *Southern Review*, 1 (Winter 1936), 522-7.

___ "Writing and Region." Lecture given at University of Tennessee-Knoxville, 19 July 1984.

Baer, Barbara. "Harriette Arnow's Chronicles of Destruction," *Nation*, 222 (31 Jan. 1976), 117-20.

Bright, Sallie and Annabel Girard. "Imagination Has Served Author Well." *Advocate-Messenger* (Danville, Ky.) 3 Oct. 1983, 1, 12.

"Historical News and Notices." *Tennessee Historical Quarterly*, 20 (Sept. 1961), 299.

Hudson, Patricia L. Unpublished interview with Harriette Simpson Arnow at Hindman Settlement School. Hindman, Ky., 6 August 1982.

Kotlowitz, Alex. "At 75, Full Speed Ahead." *Detroit News*, 4 Dec. 1983, 14+.

Miller, Danny. Interview: Harriette Arnow." *MELUS*, 9 (Summer 1982), 83-97.

Oates, Joyce Carol. "An American Tragedy." *New York Times Book Review*, 24 Jan. 1971. 2, 12.

Silberman, Eve. "Harriette Arnow: Ann Arbor's Most Acclaimed Novelist, Author of *The Dollmaker*, Shuns the Literary Scene." *Ann Arbor Observer*, March 1980, 3+.

Williams, Shirley. "Author of "Dollmaker" Comes Home to High Praise." *Louisville Courier-Journal*, 3 Oct. 1983.B5.

EVALUATING APPALACHIAN STUDIES
   Convenor: Barry Buxton, Appalachian Consortium
Regionalism and Revitalization: Towards A Comparative Perspective on Appalachian Studies
   Richard Blaustein, East Tennessee State University
The "Brier Sermon" Signpost in Appalachian Studies
   Ricky Cox, Radford University
Appalachia: A Case Study With A Look Back
   Rogers McAvoy, West Virginia University
Appalachian Educational Research in the National Context: Where We Have Been and Where We Are Going
   Alan J. DeYoung, University of Kentucky

Regionalism and Revitalization: Towards a Comparative Perspective on Appalachian Studies

by
Richard Blaustein

All of us have our own particular frames of reference, key terms and concepts which help us make sense out of the blooming, buzzing confusion of human experience. For myself, the concepts of cultural revitalization, nativism and psychosocial homeostasis have great intellectual appeal and explanatory power. I will never forget how fascinating I found anthropologist James Mooney's account of the Ghost Dance Movement among the Plains Indians in the 1890's while still an undergraduate at Brooklyn College nearly twenty-five years ago. It is only very recently, however, that I have attempted to apply these models and concepts to an intellectual and social movement with which all of us are familiar and to which all of us in this session are affiliated, that is to say, the Appalachian Studies Movement itself. Can the Appalachian Studies movement be classified as a bona fide revitalization movement? Does the application of the terminology of revitalization movement theory to the Appalachian Studies movement give us greater insight into our own personal and collective attitudes and behavior, or does it represent the imposition of an alien conceptual framework upon a social and cultural phenomenon which above all needs to be better understood in its own terms? As you can plainly see, I am anticipating the sorts of arguments which can easily emerge when one attempts to be objective and analytical about issues which also command a great deal of personal and emotional involvement. As we know, the Appalachian Studies Movement is in part an attempt to further interdisciplinary communication and cooperation between scholars drawn from a variety of academic disciplines, but it is also very much a cultural and social movement which seeks to improve the quality of life of the people of the Appalachians, particularly self-images and self-perceptions which are at best ambiguous. Accepting the precaution that no single theory or model can totally explain a phenomenon as complex as the Appalachian Studies movement, I will now proceed to discuss some fundamental features of nativistic revitalization movement theory and attempt to apply them to our own history and situation.

When we review anthropologist Ralph Linton's classic article Nativistic Movements" (*American Anthropologist*, XLV, 1943), we find that he succinctly defines a nativistic movement as "any conscious, organized attempt on the part of a society's members to revive or perpetuate selected aspects of its culture." Inherent, then in the concept of the nativistic (or revitalistic) movement is the idea that the nativistic response occurs in reaction to the perceived deterioration of an existing social and cultural order which is meaningful to its adherents. As Linton explicitly states, return to the ideal past is a powerful motivating force in nativistic movements, but in practical terms, this return must inevitably be selected and symbolic rather than total and literal: "What really happens in all nativistic movements is that certain current or remembered elements of culture are selected for emphasis and given symbolic value." A precondition, then, of the nativistic revitalization movement is the partial assimilation or acculturation of the group in question into a larger, often more powerful and prestigious cultural and social system and the emergence of the need to offset the resulting loss of sense of identity and social identity by creating new cultural symbols and social institutions which refer to but do not and cannot actually replicate the pre-modern past. Can we find concrete examples of this in the Appalachian movement? Certainly, we can, and it would not be straining our model to state that the Appalachian Studies movement is, at least in part, a rational nativistic movement. Rather than restructuring itself through magical or supernatural means, the group in question revives and/or perpetuates "symbols of a period when the society was free or, in retrospect, happy or great... by keeping the past in mind, such elements help to re-establish and maintain the self-respect of the group's members in the face of adverse conditions. Also, "they provide the society's members with a fund of common knowledge and experience which is exclusively their own and which sets them off from the members of other societies...the culture elements selected for symbolic use are chosen realistically and with regard to the possibility of perpetuating them under current conditions."

In the case of the Appalachian Studies movement, it is important to note that the impetus to revive or perpetuate selected features of the cultural heritage which symbolize the positive identity of the group not only comes from committed natives of the region but also from concerned newcomers and outsiders who have come to identify with Appalachia and its people. As we know from the works of Henry Shapiro and David Whisnant, "fotched-on women" and other well-meaning social and cultural reformers have played an undeniably influential role in the selective rediscovery and reinterpretation of the cultural past of the region. As Whisnant notes in *All Things Native and Fine* (1985), the so-called Appalachian folk revival was only part of a larger effort on the part of reformers to make mountain people bi-cultural: dulcimers and ballads were gracious accompaniments to a genteel, fundamentally middle-class American life-style; the revival aspect of the settlement schools and missionaries was essentially meant to cushion the full impact of industrial exploitation and total assimilation into the mainstream of American mass society and culture. Nominally an expression of Appalachian cultural autonomy, the Appalachian folk revival movement is more accurately described as a transcultural movement which still continues to bring together natives and newcomers within the context of new social groupings and institutions (notably folk festivals and folk schools), united by common interest in regional issues (rather than kinship or common regional background) serving as the focus of collective identity and solidarity. As we know, though, tension and conflict between native and "fotched-on" proponents of Appalachian cultural identity are real and not completely resolved factors in the Appalachian Studies movement as it has developed.

It is primarily for this reason that I fall short of defining the Appalachian Studies Movement as a completely bona fide example of a nativistic movement, though the nativistic element is real. However, Anthony F.C. Wallace's definition of a revitalization movement as a "deliberate, conscious, organized effort on the part of members of a society to create a more satisfactory culture" comes somewhat closer to explaining these particular historical developments within a general theory of sociocultural dynamics. Essentially Wallace's model of the process of cultural revitalization can be seen as a specific derivative of general systems theory. Through the comparative analysis of many revitalistic movements Wallace has isolated an irreversible series of developmental phases which characterize the revitalistic process regardless of local cultural differences; he attributes this generic uniformity to the underlying psychological and emotional attributes which all human beings share in common. All human beings seek to satisfy biological, emotional and intellectual drives, preserve a sense of meaningful connection with the natural and social worlds around them, through the particular cultural systems they have internalized. Breakdown in the effectiveness of these internalized cultural systems results in stress, which can either lead to anomie (depersonalization and disorientation) or else provide the motivation for the reinterpretation, redefinition and ideally the reorganization of the group. While many anthropologists in the past have concentrated on magically and supernaturally oriented revitalization movements, more recently we have seen more attention to rational movements, particularly those which involve the establishment of legal-rational voluntary associations which represent collective compensation for the sensed deterioration of older social and cultural patterns. Israeli social historian S.N. Eisenstadt (1968) presents the following general model of response to social change:

> In each process of change we may distinguish among: 1) the initial impetus to change and its locus in the given groups of society or in its environment; 2) the extent to which it undermines any given institutional pattern; 3) the new possibilities which are opened up by the impetus to change; and 4) the extent to which there develops within each group some ability to reorganize its social and cultural life.

The industrialization of the Southern Appalachians and the concurrent deterioration of the old subsistence-oriented life-style has essentially provided the background for the development of the Appalachian movement. In an idealized, selective, symbolic form, the old subsistence culture contrasts violently with the literate, industrialized corporate-dominated world to which modern Appalachians are compelled to adjust and adapt themselves. The development of regionally-oriented organizations helps to ease the trauma of all-out assimilation, not only for modern mountaineers but also for their counterparts in other rapidly changing societies. As the social anthropologist Robert T. Anderson has noted: "Where societies are experiencing rapid social change, formal voluntary associations typically are found." In industrial societies which are emerging from premechanical agrarian conditions, there is a need for institutions larger than the family but smaller than the state, possessing a legal-rational structure, including formal (rather than traditional) membership, charters, voting rights, etc. The revitalistic aspect of voluntary associations stems from their capacity to reduce the identity-destroying stress which comes from the breakdown or disappearance of traditional community patterns. Through ethnic or regional associations or clubs, displaced people can recreate an approximation of their old society and thus selectively preserve at least a generalized sense of distinctive group identity. As Anderson comments, "an important function of voluntary associations is their capacity at times to maintain a stable base for traditionalists resident in a non-traditional milieu." (AA, "Voluntary Associations in History," 1971:217). Such associations provide enclaves of stability for people grappling with the strains and conflicts of modernization and biculturalism. As Loyal Jones has noted in his introduction to *Minstrel of the Appalachians: The Story of Bascom Lamar Lunsford* (Appalachian Consortium Press, 1984), "...if we are to benefit from the culture that spawned us, we must carry it into new times and places." Lunsford himself was an excellent example of the revitalistic leader who understood the necessity of creating new social settings for the old culture. Rather than turning his back on the realities of modern life, he selectively balanced tradition and innovation in his folk festivals. As Loyal Jones comments:

> Bascom Lunsford found a way to strengthen the old traditions and use them to put people at ease about their place and culture at a time when most of the messages about Appalachia were negative...He helped create an atmosphere in which the folk traditions could flourish and thus where the regional people could flourish because they had regained a sense of pride. That is a work more of us should be about (1984:ix).

Clogging teams and classes, bluegrass and oldtime music festivals, quilters organizations are vehicles through which modern Appalachians are able to express their identification with the regional culture without completely rejecting modern corporate and bureaucratic life; again, since such new organizations are based on common interest rather than the traditional bonds of kinship and physical proximity, they make it possible for natives and newcomers to create new social networks which are only selectively traditional in cultural content. Thus from the raw materials of Southern mountain culture are created the symbolic bonds which tie together new trans-ethnic and trans-regional support groups. This applies not only to the Appalachian folk revival but possibly to the Appalachian Studies movement itself. Again, parallels can be found in other rapidly changing regional revitalization movements. Certainly, the development of alliances between native and outside intellectual and artistic leaders can be a natural and possibly even predictable reaction against the cultural, social and economic hegemony of the centralizing, standardizing, elitists who gravitate to capital cities. Appalachia itself may not currently be the most fashionable regional alternative to urban elitism (French Louisiana appears to have assumed that role in the 1980's will Appalachia be rediscovered again, and when will we see hillbilly equivalents of K-Paul Prudhomme, blackened redfish and Cajun Spice potato chips filling the need of the mainstream for color, flavor and roots?), but if the past is a reliable guide to the future, we can safely predict that modern people will continue to need the emotional security and stability which gives rise to regional revitalization movements not only here but throughout much of the contemporary world. Central to all of these movements is the idea of the idealized homeplace, the magical kingdom in which humanity is in balance with nature, unsullied by the pressures of modern corporate industrial life. The ceremonies, rituals and artforms which provide the cultural focus of regional revitalization movements enable their participants to retreat, at least temporarily, into a realm in which there is stability, order and harmony. As Yi-Fu Tuan notes in his conclusion to *Tonophilia* (means "love of place" in Greek),

Human beings have persistently searched for the ideal environment. How it looks varies from one culture to another but in essence it seems to draw on two antipodal images: the garden of innocence and the cosmos. The fruits of the earth provide security as also does the harmony of the stars which offers, in addition, grandeur. So we move from one to the other; from the shade under the baobab to the magic circle under heaven; from home to purlic square, from suburb to city; from a seaside holiday to the enjoyment of the sophisticated arts, seeking for a point of equilibrium which is not of this world. (1974:248).

It is the search to regain the safe and good place which motivates many people involved in Appalachian Studies and comparable movements. Obviously, this is not merely a physical place we are talking about, but a state of being and feeling at home with supportive others, attaining what the anthropologist Francis L.K. Hsu refers to as "psychosocial homeostasis." Just as all living beings seek to preserve and perpetuate themselves, so do all human beings seek to attain psychosocial homeostasis through contact with the persons, things, places and cultural practices towards which they feel intimate emotional attachment and involvement. It is through these intimate emotional attachments that we derive psychological and emotional stability and well-being. Changes which threaten these relationships threaten our own sense of self, and consequently Hsu believes that we can best understand the dynamics of cultural change and stability by examining the particular social and cultural symbols upon which individual and collective identity is based:

> All peoples will offer greater resistance to change in relationships and other elements in their society and culture most relevant to the maintenance of psychosocial homeostasis than in other relationships and elements. They will offer greater resistance to change in those areas because they have invested strong affect, but not where they are mere role players or spectators. (1971:36)

My own research in this regard has focused primarily on music, but clearly we can see the search for the good, safe place expressing itself in many other forms, genres and media, including scholarly research and criticism. Indeed, the establishment and perpetuation of an institution like the Appalachian Studies Conference itself could be considered a regionally oriented expression of what is actually a universal human drive. As I said at the beginning of this essay, no single theory or model can ever *completely* explain a phenomenon as complex as the Appalachian Studies Movement. I do hope, however, that some of the ideas I have presented here will help to encourage further considerations of the need for a comparative perspective in Appalachian Studies.

NOTES

Anderson, Robert T., "Voluntary Associations in History," *American Anthropologist*, vol. 73, no. 1, 1971.

Eisenstadt, S.N. (ed.), *Comparative Perspectives on Social Change*, Boston: Little, Brown & Co., 1968.

Hsu, Francis L.K., "Psychosocial Homeostasis and Jen: Conceptual Tools For Advancing Psychological Anthropology." *American Anthropologist*, vol. 73, no. 1, 1971.

Jones, Loyal, *Minstrel of the Appalachians: The Story of Bascom Lamar Lunsford*. Boone, N.C.: Appalachian Consortium Press, 1984.

Linton, Ralph, "Nativistic Movements," *American Anthropologist*, vol. 45, no. 2, 1943.

Tuan, Yi-Fu, *Topophilia: A Study of Environmental Perception, Attitudes and Values*. Englewood Cliffs, N.J.: Prentice-Hall, Inc., 1974.

Wallace, Anthony F.C., "Revitalization Movements: Some Theoretical Considerations For Their Comparative Study," *American Anthropologist*, vol. 58, no. 2, 1956.

The "Brier Sermon," Signpost in Appalachian Studies

by
Ricky Cox

When I transferred from a community college to Radford University three years ago, I didn't know that there was such a thing as an Appalachian Studies Program there or anywhere else. But since then, Appalachian Studies has become possibly the single most important element in my education, though not in the sense that I would choose for myself a career founded on it. But the realization that there is no life work here for me in no way detracts from the value of the experiences Appalachian Studies has brought to me, for while these experiences cannot guarantee the prosperity of my future, they certify the value of my past. That may not sound like much, and some might think that I, and others like me, have been spending our time and money buying back things that were ours to start with. Maybe so, and I will come back to this topic, the past, a little later. But for now, bear with me as I suggest to you that this is a ransom worth paying.

In doing so I wish to discuss, in a very unstructured way, the role of the Appalachian Studies Conference in bringing together parties who wish to traffic in this business. And finally, I would like to tie this all together through discussion of selected ideas from a poem by Jim Wayne Miller, entitled, "Brier Sermon-You Must Be Born Again." While I find this piece well-suited to my purpose, I did not actively choose it; it volunteered. Not long after enrolling at Radford, I became acquainted with Dr. Grace Toney Edwards, Chair of the Appalachian Studies Program there. We talked at length about Appalachian related issues of current concern to me. One day she gave me a copy of "Brier Sermon-You Must Be Born Again," with several passages highlighted. I read in those few lines a clear, concise expression of my own worries and concerns. Since then "Brier Sermon" has turned up over and over in classroom materials and in informal discussions and each time I find myself mentally underlining something new. At each fork and turn in the road, it tells the traveller where he has been and where he is going, linking the way back with the way ahead. It marks each direction clearly, yet binds them into one unbroken passage, reminding us constantly, like a signpost, that all roads are somehow connected, and that wherever we would go, we can get there from here.

Many of you will be familiar with this piece either alone, or as a part of the volume of poetry in which it appears, *The Mountains Have Come Closer*. It is a long poem, so I will not read it to you, but I will give you, at least, the setting of "Brier Sermon-You Must Be Born Again." Do not worry if you are not familiar with this work for once you have heard the Brier's message you will, I think discover that, like Dorothy Gale of Kansas, you knew it all along.

The book, *The Mountains Have Come Closer*, is divided into three parts, the third of which is called simply, "Brier Sermon." In it we see, through the eyes of a narrator, a man who leaves the mountains to find work in a big city. He finds himself trapped in a stereotyped mold outside of which he cannot be accepted by mainstream America. We see this man, a Brier he is called by the sophisticated city dwellers, back home, moving about in his own world, seeing it attacked and despoiled from without, and corroded and neglected from within. We come to know the Brier as a sensitive, thoughtful man, but we do not hear him speak until the last poem in this part three. This poem is "Brier Sermon-You Must Be Born Again," and it begins with this introduction: "One Friday night the Brier felt called to preach. So Saturday morning, early, he appeared on a street corner in town and started preaching, walking up and down the sidewalk...He took as his text, 'You Must Be Born Again'"(Miller 52). This theme, you must be born again, is repeated constantly throughout the poem, or sermon, and I jump to the final pages of the Brier's message to pull out his definition of that idea. "What's it like - being born again?/ It's going back to what you were before/ without losing what you've since become" (Miller 63). Here in two lines is the essence of what Appalachian Studies may offer to natives of the region especially, but also to anyone else who is looking for pieces of themselves lost or misplaced along the road to somewhere else.

One of the first things the Brier talks about in relation to this theme is education. He tells a story about two families, the Johnsons and the Browns, who represent two extremes of what we commonly think of as being educated. Asked to dig up some cedar trees, the Johnson boys base their refusal on an old superstition. "Get old Jim Brown and Tom Brown," they say. "They're educated, don't believe in nothin" (Miller 52). Writers sometimes set up exaggerated contrasts to make a point, but in this case the polarization is not inconsistent with real attitudes about what it means to be "educated." The uneducated Johnson boys are bound by superstition and conduct themselves in accordance with traditions and beliefs that defy rational explanation. The educated Browns don't accept anything on the basis of faith alone. They exemplify the educational ideal that one should accept only what one can verify for himself. Inherited experience of the past has no place in their lives.

Somehow, we have come to tolerate the idea that, like Jim and Tom Brown, we must first shed off the past like the skin of a snake before we can fully participate in the future. The process is regrettable, but inevitable as the values and basic assumptions of rural society must topple in the face of scholarship and inquiry. Is it strange, then, that many Appalachians in colleges and universities have difficulty making connections between experiences of the past and expectations for the future? Pressured by active persuasion at school and passive acceptance at home, the will to question and resist is easily pushed aside by more immediate concerns. It is a hard fight to fight, yet many do it, finally achieving a balance that is workable, though it may entail a complicated and sometimes stressful game of role playing. Too many, though, cannot deal with a dual identity and reject one position or the other. Sadly, this firm choice is less satisfactory than indecision. Denying ourselves the sense of place offered by home ties, or the intellectual adrenalin of pursuits attached to, or dependent upon, formal education may result in resentment of the people and ideals that force us to choose. We may become cynical, and like the Brown boys, find that we "don't believe in nothin."

The Brier would have us seek a middle ground. He says, "Well, I'm educated, but not like the Brown boys./ There's something I believe in:/ You must be born again" (Miller 53). His definition of being born again is especially pertinent to education: "It's going back to what you were before/ without losing what you've since become" (Miller 63). To do that, we need connections, bridges, between past and present. We can have them, make them. They can start out as little foot paths cut in a high school folklore project and grow into a network that crosses the country. These are roads and bridges built of thought and emotion, and unlike their counterparts of steel and asphalt, they thrive on heavy traffic. They can stretch and expand until they become mental interstates that traverse time and space.

We as individuals can build and maintain these roads, and at journey's end each must necessarily turn up his own lane or hollow. But there is a need for guides and explorers who would mark the way for the less adventuresome. That need has been, and is being met by Appalachian Studies Programs. Again, these roads are of value only when they pass by personal landmarks, but there is a need for a coordinating organization through which individuals can share ideas and accomplishments, and draw strength from others who share their concerns. There are obstacles that the individual cannot always overcome, such as the educational dilemma pointed to by the Brier. There are rivers fed by stereotype and public opinion that are not easily bridged, and I suggest to you that the Appalachian Studies Conference fulfills its brightest hopes and finest purpose in serving as a ferry between shores of differing ideals. I suggest to you also that the masters of this craft must maintain friendly relations with both sides of any stream it may cross, yet not ally itself too closely with either. I suggest also that the passengers on this craft must not let it be obsoleted by shoddy toll bridges thrown up by either side, whose builders exact some price in exchange for passage.

This is a tall order, I know, but it is not a call to arms. It is a description of what is, as much as it is a vision of what should be. And it is an outline for being as much as it is a plan for doing. In fact, I really don't know what the Appalachian Studies Conference does beyond putting on this meeting, which I have come to see as sort of a company picnic for the maintenance crews of those roads I was talking about a while ago. Do not take me wrong. I know that much hard work is being done every day, but I am speaking from the perspective that doing is an outgrowth of being and therefore secondary to it.

Being is of first importance and the value of the Appalachian Studies Conference lies in who and what it is.

It has been suggested to me that the Appalachian Studies Conference is unique among organizations of similar scope and intent in that its membership includes both scholars and artists, thinkers and feelers. We have them gathered here in the same room, and in many cases, in the same person. The value of this fortunate circumstance is related to the important idea of making connections. Those who embody both types become living connections between the academic and the aesthetic. Because their work is thoughtful in both a creative and a critical sense they can apply broader insights to either kind of project. In drawing upon the past as a resource they are better able to realize the need to be selective in choosing which elements of it should be brought out into the sunlight and which should be left to fade into obscurity. The Brier illustrates this need in the form of a question:

> Say you were going on a trip
> knowing you wouldn't ever be coming back
> and all you'd ever have of that place you knew,
> that place where you'd always lived
> was what you could take with you.
> You'd want to think what to take along
> what would travel well
> what you'd really need and wouldn't need.
> I'm telling you, every day you're leaving
> a place you won't be coming back to ever.
> What are you going to leave behind?
> What are you taking with you?
> Don't run off and leave the best part of yourself.
> (Miller 59)

This process of selection and occasional resorting of cultural baggage is not an easy one, but it can be worthwhile. Many of the best examples of Appalachian scholarship and creativity attest to a compromise on the part of the author that allows him or her to draw strength and material from experiences that predate becoming "educated," yet do so more effectively through the enhanced fluency of phrase and clarity of thought that may be the finest things a formal education has to offer. While these people do not pine for the good old days, they remember the past and recognize it as a part of today, and as a part of them, wherever they go, whatever they do. They make connections and build bridges.

Some will call this respect for the past a crutch. They say it is nostalgia with a necktie on, masquerading as scholarship. They say that backward people want to live in the past because the future is bleak or frightening. I couldn't say whether or not this is so, but I do know that even when the future holds only promise, there is value in looking back. The Brier talks about it in his sermon. "Our foreparents left us a very fine inheritance,/ but we don't believe it" (Miller 53). "'We're ashamed to live in our father's house./ We think it's too old-fashioned" (Miller 53). Now where would this inheritance be found? Not in the bank or the top bureau drawer. It's in the past. It's in the words and wants and dreams of our mothers and fathers and grandparents. Think about those little hilltop cemeteries scattered through the mountains and think about going there at odd intervals, maybe in the rain. Remember to turn off your lights and try not to get your feet wet. Take a minute when it's time to leave because you're blocked in anyway. Take a minute and look at the names you see there. Look at the dates. They are two inches apart, yet a lifetime lies between them. Wonder about these people. Wonder what they wondered about. Make connections. On your way down the hill, pick up a rock and put in in your pocket and carry it home with you.

Now maybe you are thinking, "This is nice, but we need direction for the future, not a map of the past." That is true, and recognition of that need is reflected in the theme of this meeting. Along with remembrance and reunion, there is revival, a gathering of strength and purpose for what is to come. And like the organizers of the conference, the Brier is aware of the need for continuity, for a connection between past, present, and future. He warns his sidewalk congregation:

> But you don't have to live in the past.
> You can't, even if you try.
> You don't have to talk old-fashioned,
> dress old-fashioned.
> You don't have to live the way your foreparents lived.
> But if you don't know about them
> if you don't love them
> if you don't respect them
> you're not going anywhere.
> You don't have to think ridge-to-ridge,
> the way they did.
> You can think ocean-to-ocean. (Miller 55)

Before ending, I want to return to the Brier's original topic, education, for three reasons. First, I know that many people involved with Appalachian Studies are associated in some way with formal education. Second, I want to suggest that we in Appalachia are not the only ones guilty of the sin of forgetfulness, especially in the field of education. And third, I want to satisfy a personal penchant for connectedness.

The first of these reasons is self-explanatory. The second recalls an assumption I spoke of a while ago. The notion that being educated demands that we reject our personal history is closely related to the idea that our collective history is not an essential element of education. Many of us have come to equate progress with technology and material gain and have drawn the false conclusion that since we have more than did our predecessors in these respects, then we must be more intelligent. We become disdainful of the wisdom of the past, thinking that it no longer applies. The Liberal Arts give the lie to the assumption that each generation is unique in its thought and motivation and is possessed of a finer insight than were the thinkers of the past. History and literature can teach us that human nature remains constant regardless of change in the human condition. We are no more at risk as a people who reject two hundred years of cultural heritage than we are as a nation who neglects two thousand years of Western Civilization. And I suggest to you that if we manage to turn ourselves around, Appalachia will find itself standing out in front instead of racing to catch up, for we already possess the quality most needed to make sense of our lives and our world. That characteristic is the desire and need to see connections between concepts and ideas and to put abstract things into concrete terms. In an essay entitled "A Mirror for Appalachia" Jim Wayne Miller discusses this quality at length along with the Appalachian tendency to respond more quickly to feelings than to ideas. He quotes Jack Weller who said, "The problem is that our educational system is based on ideas, not feelings." Miller then asks, "That is the problem, but whose problem is it, ultimately" (450)? This is a thought provoking question and I want to apply it specifically to the concept of connectedness.

I think that some of you will share my belief that the ability to make connections of all types must be the chief benefit of a Liberal Arts education. To perceive some pattern in the infinite diversity of the world is to make it a friendlier, less confusing place. It should be an advantage, then, to have this habit of making connections already in place, and I suggest to you that if there is one quality attributed to Appalachians by critics and proponents alike, it is a preoccupation, some would say an obsession, with connections. I offer two examples.

The first is the sometimes derided recognition of extended kinship. Friend and foe alike have hung all kinds of interpretations on the emphasis Appalachians place on genealogy, but if nothing else, it is a clear demonstration of the need to establish and maintain connections.

The second example I would refer you to is speech. The media delight in mocking the picturesque speech of the mountaineer and some people seem to equate a reliance on simile and metaphor with the inability to grasp complex or abstract notions. While this is not necessarily a lie, neither is it necessarily the truth. Rather than indicating that a speaker or writer has fallen short of comprehension, an appropriate analogy may demonstrate that he has gone a step further and related the idea to something already within his range of experience. I would even suggest to you that judicious use of concrete images in exploring abstract ideas is nothing short of homespun scholarship. Without benefit or burden of page number and copyright, the speaker refers his audience to a chapter in their common experience and says, in effect, "Do not take my word for it. Let me refer you to a better authority. My source is experience and life itself." If we would heed the Brier's message we would have as a resource not only the incomplete volume of our own lives, but also the great reference library that is the past.

I make here a final point about the value of "Brier Sermon-You Must Be Born Again." Not only do the Brier and his creator, Jim Wayne Miller, give direction on this road, they travel along with us as well in that this poem and many others by this author exemplify the use of these sometimes neglected resources. The Brier Sermon is rich in metaphor: You must be born again; live in your father's house; and, you can be old wine in a new bottle. My favorite is addressed to young hot rodders. The Brier tells how he sees them flat on their backs, "looking up into the guts and gears of America," and thinks to himself:

> I'd like to open up your heads
> just like you raise the hood or go into a gearbox.
> I'd like to re-wire your heads
> and gap your spark plugs and re-set your timing.
>
> Because you can get off your back
> you can have a new view
> you can get behind the wheel of America.
> You can sit in the smooth upholstered seats of power
> and listen to the music playing. (Miller 57-58)

Now, metaphors about roses have their place, but it's hard to beat the smooth upholstered seats of power.

I want to end now, as I started, with a personal note. I am a machinist by trade and I like my work. I continued at it part time while attending college and was at first frustrated by my inability to make any connection between what seemed like two entirely different worlds. In my second year at Radford I took a course in Appalachian Folklore. On the syllabus for that course was a list of "opportunities." At first I thought this was just a tongue-in-cheek way to say requirements. I will say now that the folklore project done as a part of that class was truly an opportunity. I did my project on machines in folklore, and for the first time was able to make connections between iron and steel and paper and pen. I interviewed people around home who share my passion for machinery and looked through scholarly articles and books concerning industrialization. While the result is no more than average as such things go, I see it as the best thing I did in my entire time at Radford because it gave me the chance to make connections and build bridges between different parts of my life and thereby feel better about each of them. I do not know that everyone would benefit from a similar experience, but I am grateful that

Appalachian Studies provided me with that wonderful opportunity. I want to thank, also, Jim Wayne Miller and the many others like him who show us that the road runs in two directions.

WORKS CITED

Miller, Jim Wayne. "A Mirror for Appalachia." *Voices From the Hills*. Eds. Robert J. Higgs and Ambrose N. Manning. New York: Frederick Ungar Publishing Co., 1975.

"Brier Sermon-You Must Be Born Again." *The Mountains Have Come Closer*. Boone, North Carolina: Appalachian Consortium Press, 1980.

Educational Research in the National Context: Where We Have Been and Where We Are Going

by
Alan J. DeYoung

Research and scholarship on educational issues and trends in Appalachia, at least that performed by educators themselves and specifically targeted at regional concerns, has been virtually non-existent. Thus, to the question about where Appalachian educational research has been, the easy answer must be "nowhere". Suc h an assessment should not be taken as an indictment of the quality of regional scholarship. As I will argue shortly, regional and rural educational issues in Appalachia and elsewhere have received little specific attention throughout the history of American education. And the lack of concern shown by educational researchers towards Appalachian educational issues and problems in actuality indicates more about the political nature of school reform in the U.S., and the conceptual inadequacies which have historically undergirded educational research community pursuits, than it does about the quality and/or integrity of regional writers.

The Urban Focus of Nineteenth Century American Education

Rather than dwelling in this essay on the important Appalachian education topics and questions not pursued by professional educators, I would like to frame my discussion of this phenomenon within the larger underdevelopment of rural schooling scholarship in the U.S. During the past two decades, a number of educational historians have become quite interested in America's clearly urban bias in questions of educational research and policy. As several of them note, most of the late nineteenth century school reform literature focused on ways of coordinating and administering education in urban environments. Virtually all leaders of the common school movement during this period were urban school superintendents whose careers essentially depended upon the bureaucratization and professionalization of urban education (Perkinson, 1968; Tyack and Hansot, 1982).

Models of rural education in fact became the primary enemy of many nineteenth century school reformers, who argued that the politics, inefficiency, and uncoordinated curricular characteristics of rural schools could never serve as a model for the institutionalization of public education in the U.S. Because America's cities were quickly becoming inundated with hordes of new immigrants, because the new technologies emerging in the workplace demanded the teaching of different types of vocational skills, and because advances in the "science" of administration clearly showed the inefficiency of parent control of educational policy, proponents of schooling structures and procedures which had worked earlier in rural settings were quickly outflanked in America's major cities by school superintendents who argued that they had a better way. Eventually, supporters of autonomous rural schools outside of America's urban areas also suffered defeat during the late nineteenth century as urban reformers with their calls for more efficient schooling systematically infiltrated state departments of public education and pressed for sweeping reforms in the way schools were organized, staffed, and supervised.

By the beginning of the twentieth century, most Americans and their leaders had become convinced of two things. First, that the country's future lay in its continued urbanization and industrialization. And second, that America's emerging institutional leaders (including school administrators) could and/or would solve whatever technical and social problems emerged from future urban and economic development. For many American educators, the educational problem of the twentieth century was an urban problem. As educational reformers like John Dewey and I.W. Howerth argued, progress in education depended upon the recreation of community in America's urban areas for the multitude of children who had never experienced its many benefits. While the old rural villages in America would supposedly continue to decline in the face of the advances in science and industrialization, the practical, moral, and applied experiences of community vocational and moral life which rural living earlier provided children needed to be incorporated and in fact made central in the mission of twentieth century city schools (Perkinson, 1968). On the other hand, rural schools themselves were found inadequate by various spokespersons favoring the "new" education by the turn of the century. "Administrative progressives" found rural schools poorly organized and inefficiently administered and curricular progressives found the haphazard focus on works of Western civilization not vocationally or scientifically sound enough for the future roles rural students might play in whatever community and national contexts they might end up in.

Educational Research and Educational Policy in the Early TwentiethCentury

By current standards, most of the policy discussions and decisions regarding small and rural schools of the early twentieth century were not guided by empirical research, but came as the result of convictions state departments of education had about making rural districts more professional, efficient, and in many cases vocationally relevant (Rosenfeld and Sher, 1977). In many ways, developments in rural vocational educational policy mirrored those of agricultural policy during this century. As several authors suggest, the "Country Life" movement of the early twentieth century articulated the restoration of declining rural life in the U.S. via scientifically enhancing agricultural practices among American farmers and making rural schools more vocationally relevant to the emerging industrial needs of the United States. Through demonstration projects and "technical assistance" to public school curriculum developers, U. S. Department of Agriculture Extension Agents (among others) had an important influence on rural public schools throughout the twentieth century, and especially after the passage of the Smith-Hughes Act of 1917 (Grantham, 1983; Greenwood, 1982).

Perhaps the earliest forms of what scholars would now recognize as educational research on specific rural schooling problems were the "school surveys" of the early twentieth century. These statistical profiles were typically utilized by educational reformers to "improve" rural schools by first documenting their comparatively inferior status, and then helping to bring them under the control of state superintendents of education (Tyack, 1974). Many progressive educators during this period called for and achieved reform in the professional training of teachers and school consolidation, the latter innovation which would ostensibly allow for more efficient utilization of financial resources and age grading of students (DeYoung and Boyd, 1987; Tyack and Hansot, 1982).

Small schools in particular were often targeted for reform throughout the early twentieth century, not necessarily because they were shown deficient pedagogically, but because they were assumed to be less intellectually stimulating environments and certainly were less desirable administratively and financially.

> (the) movement to take control of the rural common school away from the local community and to turn it over to the professionals was part of a more general organizational revolution in American education in which laymen lost much of their direct control over the schools. In the cities school men pioneered new bureaucratic patterns of educational organization. They (also) sought to "free education from politics" by coercing rural communities to consolidate schools. From 1910 to 1960 the number of one room schools declined from approximately 200,000 to 20,000. (Tyack, 1974 p.25)

In addition to school surveys, three other types of educational research were prominent during the first fifty years of the twentieth century. The first of these focused upon ways of actually making schools more administratively efficient and bureaucratic as desired by state and district superintendents. Relatedly, quasi-empirical accounts of innovative techniques in cost-effective materials and supervision practices were sponsored by educational professionals convinced that the future of school improvement lay in improved management techniques (Callahan, 1962). And finally, the field of eugenics had an interest in rural school populations of several small isolated regions of the U.S., particularly Appalachia. The majority of scholars writing in this area were convinced that many rural schools were heavily populated by cognitively deficient children whose parents had not been smart enough or fortunate enough to leave the decaying countryside for the more lucrative and stimulating environments of America's cities. Because many rural children scored poorly on early standardized tests of ability, such data were typically cited as further evidence that not only were many of America's rural residents lacking in intelligence, but that rural life patterns not "upgraded" by the intervention of outside influences would continue to erode in the future (e.g. Hirsch, 1928; Key, 1932; Silver and DeYoung, 1985).

School and Community Studies in the "Non-professional" Literature

As this review so far indicates, empirical educational research into the particular problems and needs of America's small and rural schools well into the twentieth century was sparse and ideologically motivated, since the development of American education as a whole was built upon the assumption that schools of the future would and should continue to become larger, more efficient, and more vocationally relevant. To be sure, some rural educators were convinced early in the century that inequality and discrimination existed in particular regions of the country. However, their calls for national research and compensatory educational policies were continually rebuffed by federal legislators unwilling to interfere with state and local control of public education (Ravitch, 1983).

On the other hand, there have been several types of informative studies on issues, problems, and strengths of rural schools which originated outside of the educational research community but which have anticipated some of the current interest in rural and Appalachian education. In particular, the field of community studies became prominent in the 1930s and 1940s, and more academic interpretations of the centrality of the public school in the lives of continuing rural communities have been intimately detailed by a variety of social historians and community sociologists (e.g. Lynd and Lynd, 1937; Warner and Lunt, 1941). More recently (and with a more sympathetic orientation) Peshkin has focused on the importance of small town schools for community identity (Peshkin 1978; Peshkin 1982). As well, the potential of local rural schools to help rebuild and/or enhance disappearing community cohesiveness has been illustrated and advocated by Eliot Wigginton, who is also specifically interested in Appalachian education (Puckett, 1986; Wigginton, 1985).

Of late, a number of educational historians have also been particularly interested in re-telling the battle of school consolidation as seen from the perspective of local populations. Fuller, for example, has provided an excellent discussion of local citizen efforts in a number of mid-western states to resist and/or modify national forces of school consolidation early in the twentieth century. Importantly, debates over strengths, weaknesses, problems and solutions to those problems discussed in much of the early school consolidation literature are still central to current discourse on school reform in rural education. In a sense then, the significance and importance of the rural school in American community life has been well recognized and researched by sociologists and historians for decades, but only recently has surfaced among educational researchers unfortunately unfamiliar with the legacy of these debates.

The Current Status of Rural Educational Research

Current interest in the specific problems and possibilities of rural education seems to have come about for at least four types of reasons. Initially, it has become apparent to educational policy makers that even though significant out-migration from farms and small towns has occurred during the past century, such trends have slowed greatly during the past two decades, and in some cases have been reversed (Beale, 1975; Sher, 1981). Thus, all rural schools and their particular problems will not be completely disappearing in the foreseeable future. In addition, concern over equality of educational opportunity in rural areas became an important issue in the 1970s, and a growing body of literature suggests that problems of minority and special needs rural students have frequently not been adequately met by urban based models of service delivery (Helge, 1981; Massey and Crosby, 1983). As well, much of the current national interest in "effective schooling" has questioned the conventional wisdom that bigger schools and more centralized staffing patterns are always desirable (Goodlad, 1984; Sher, 1986). And finally, the current interest in improving rural education as an aid to stimulating local economic development within a number of states seems related to more concerted efforts among such states to upgrade rural schools (Rosenfeld, 1983; DeYoung and Boyd, 1987).

The current generation of scholarship on the particular issues and problems of rural education in the U.S. was ushered in by the work of Jonathan Sher and several of his colleagues in the late 1970s and early 1980s. Perhaps the landmark book on the overlooked importance of rural education and the lack of relevant scholarship in this area was Sher's edited collection of 1977. Suggestively entitled *Education in Rural America: A Reasesssment of Convention-*

al Wisdom, the book's major accomplishment was not primarily to document all that is known about the strengths and weaknesses of rural schools, but instead to show that policy makers and researchers actually knew very little about rural education in the U.S., due to the "urbanization of rural schools" perspectives suggested so far in this essay. Other chapters of the Sher book (which included educational dynamics in some Appalachian states) focused upon and illustrated several fallacies of the "conventional wisdom" about rural schools by: documenting the myth of economy, efficiency and equality supposedly brought to rural regions of the country by school consolidation and centralization efforts; examining both the conceptual weaknesses *and* benefits associated with small schools in rural regions of the country; and questioning the desirability of equating increased financial support of local public schools with the erosion of local autonomy in school decision making. In addition, several case studies illustrating the politics of school reform and the importance of understanding class conflict in rural educational issues were included.

The scholarship which has most recently emerged specifically on ruralness and the particular concerns of rural communities and educators can be put into four interrelated categories. These include: an interest in the status of minority and handicapped children in rural regions of the U.S.; research and commentary about ongoing financial, curricular, and staffing problems many small schools are facing today in an educational environment driven by the needs of metropolitan school districts; general attempts to conceptually and/or empirically define or construct research agendas for rural and small school education based on literature reviews and or surveys of rural educators; and several attempts to discuss educational reform in the context of community economic development.

Equality of Educational Opportunity in Rural America

A slow-to-develop nationally relevant motivation behind renewed interest in rural schooling in the United States has been the re-discovery of poverty and inequality in many rural regions of the country, particularly Appalachia. The early "Children of Crisis" series by Robert Coles, for example, graphically and eloquently portrayed lives of disadvantaged black, chicano, indian and white children in the deep south, among migrant farm populations, and in the mining regions of the United States (Coles, 1967; 1970; 1972). As well, Michael Harrington's provocative essay on *The Other America* (1962), and David Looff's book *Appalachia's Children* (1971) also suggested that many rural as well as urban children lacked fundamental opportunities in this country.

Bridging the gap between poverty and the public school in the national literature however received much less early attention in rural America than it did in urban areas. For example, "activist" teacher memoirs of degrading educational conditions in the public schools of the 1960s by authors like Dennison (1969), Herndon (1968), Kohl (1967) and Kozol (1967) were all *urban* chronicles. With the possible exception of Conroy's *The Water is Wide* (1972), tales of rural school deprivation never captured much national attention.

According to some, most of the quality educational research on issues and problems in rural schooling has been done by educational anthropologists interested in the particular problems of educating various black, migrant, hispanic, and/or indian populations primarily in the south, southwest or Alaska. Typically, much of this work was done under the framework of understanding culturally different populations rather than aspects of ruralness per se, yet observations and analyses found in these works seem still the most useful for understanding many of the dynamics of school and community relationships in rural America (e.g. Precourt, 1982; Wax, Wax and Dumont, 1964; Spindler, 1977).

Shirley Brice Heath (1983), for example, has studied and written on communication patterns and community life among two rural piedmont communities in the Carolinas. Based on her extensive fieldwork in these settings, she argued that compared to children from "townspeople" families, children she studied varied greatly with regard to the activities and language skills needed to succeed in school. For one of her communities, she argued,

> The sequence of habits Trackton children develop in learning language, telling stories, making metaphors, and seeing patterns across items and events do not fit the developmental patterns of either linguistic or cognitive growth reported in the literature on mainstream children. (p. 343)

Perhaps the only state which has historically addressed problems of ethnic communities and rural issues in education has been Alaska. For example, Barnhardt (1977; 1982) edited two volumes on "Cross-Cultural Issues in Alaskan Education" which contained descriptions, critiques and analyses of existing and developing educational programs there. As well, Kleinfeld (1972) published an important study on teacher effectiveness variables with Eskimo and indian secondary school students. According to some, Alaska's early recognition that it would never be populous or urban has led to growing patterns of local control and administrative decentralization, and to more serious attention to educational policy issues attendant to ruralness, isolation, and economic development than has been the case in the rest of the country (Hecht, 1981).

While much of the best scholarship on rural educational conditions has dealt extensively with self-contained minority populations in the U.S. and/or their problematic contact with the majority culture, more recent literature on rural education issues has focused on the defacto discrimination of rural minorities viz. compensatory programs which urban minorities are claimed to enjoy (e.g., De La Garza, 1979; Fratoe, 1978). Many of the current rural education activists have seemingly been attracted to this area by what they perceive to be the inequality of educational opportunity afforded handicapped populations in rural schools (Helge, 1981; Huebner, Cummings and McLesky, 1985). Central to most of their discussions is the purported inability of some rural schools to deliver special services for the handicapped and/or other special need student populations due to state and federal funding formulas which make diagnosis and intervention strategies difficult. That is, while mandated state and federal programs for special needs children in metropolitan districts can at least be moderately successful when schools share or rotate specialists, isolated rural districts frequently cannot share resources nearly as effectively. Typically, scholarship on this theme then takes one of two forms, either discussions of staffing needs and problems and/or calls for creative funding to better facilitate the needs of rural special populations (e.g., Huebner and Huberty, 1984; Trenary, 1980).

Issues in the Staffing, Administration and Funding of Rural Schools

Much current policy research and policy debate among rural education scholars focuses on staffing, administrative, and financing problems of rural schools in the U.S. For example, a number of authors have discussed the difficulty of attracting, training, and rewarding rural school teachers. In general, these studies suggest that teachers choosing to teach in rural areas have somewhat different occupational interests, perceive characteristics of their teaching situations somewhat differently, and may need different types of occupational incentives to keep them on the job than do teachers in metropolitan areas (e.g., Mathes and Carlson, 1986; Reed and Busby 1985). Some of this literature either documents or persuasively argues that the rural school teacher may need much more awareness of school/community relationships and either more general curricular preparation and/or a second specialization in small school districts and/or schools (Gjelten, 1978; Horn et.al, 1985; Nachtigal, 1980). There is also great concern in parts of the rural personnel preparation literature for the lack of interest many teacher training institutions place on rural school teacher education (Horn, 1983; Muse, 1977).

Discussions of providing equality of educational opportunity to economically disadvantaged populations and special needs students also typically turn to funding and administrative problems in the rural school literature. As a number of researchers have pointed out, school expenditures and resources in many rural school districts have different patterns than in metropolitan districts. For example, because many rural districts contain disproportionate numbers of economically disadvantaged students and have fewer local resources for education, funding formulas for rural school districts are frequently complicated, and the subject of continuing national and state departments of education debate. For example, in some states per pupil expenditures for instruction in rural districts have been shown to be lower than expenditures in metropolitan districts (DeYoung, 1985a; Rosenfeld, 1981), while costs for transportation and capital outlay have been much higher (Guthrie, 1979; Thompkins, 1977). Studies attempting to statistically document best ways of financing economically disadvantaged rural schools indicate that their diversity makes such general questions very difficult to answer in economic terms (Butler and Monk, 1985; Guthrie, 1979). For example, Rosenfeld (1981) argues that most research on rural schools, patterns of rural student achievement and educational opportunity have been performed at the school district level. However, while districts in some primarily rural states follow county boundaries, in other states school districts are based on townships, and in others both types of districts exist. Noting that comprehensive educational research at the school building level has yet to be performed, he argues that at best we need to know much more about school building dynamics before sound rural school policies can be implemented. In the meantime, he finds it ironic that because some rural school districts cannot meet state and federal guidelines in some programmatic areas, they typically find consolidation into bigger units a necessary fact of life even though the surrounding community may feel that the existing school arrangement promotes their view of educational excellence.

Linking the conceptual and empirical discussions of "best ways" to finance rural school programs have been administrative and political struggles throughout this century. Among school administrators and state departments of education, the rural school problem during this period often focused on the composition, scale, and funding of "intermediate units (Cooper and Fitzwater, 1954). Significantly, the issue of ruralness seems entwined with "problems of smallness in American education is suggested by Rosenfeld:

> Size, of course, has implications for the number of programs and courses that can be supported in an area. It is also a major determinant of qualification for federal programs and inclusion in federal data gathering efforts. Many federal programs are targeted at population centers so that they may reach the maximum number of recipients. Consequently, many rural schools, districts and counties are too small to be funded. (1981, p.4)

No discussion of the rural education literature would be complete without some overview of the school size debate which has historically and is currently a major theme in most if not all of the rural education literature. As indicated previously, the conventional wisdom among school administrators has been that bigger school units were almost always to be desired. Bigger schools, the claim has typically been, provide for more teacher specialization, course diversity, and cost effective supervision and materials acquisition. Perhaps the last important effort to prove that larger (secondary) schools were better schools was accomplished by James Conant in 1959. According to that work, more educative high schools were those whose graduating class had at least 100 students. However, many rural citizen groups, rural school spokespersons, and several national authorities have renewed their critique of the "bigger is better" theme.

While the century-long effort to consolidate most rural public schools became a real possibility after improved road construction in the 1940s and 1950s, the energy crisis of the 1970s and ever-present poor winter weather conditions in many states put limits on total school consolidation. Practically speaking, a number of studies have suggested that transportation and administration costs in many rural regions of the country tend to mitigate against school consolidation beyond a certain point.

Similarly, just as some states have begun to accept the limitations of school consolidation in terms of cost effectiveness, several important studies have suggested the pedagogical limitations of large schools (e.g., Goodlad, 1984). Some authors, for example, have questioned the data used in the Conant study and his interpretation of them (Sher and Tompkins, 1977). Others contend that while there may be most effective minimum school sizes, there is probably a maximum one too (Goodlad, 1984). Barker and Gump (1964), for example, demonstrated that smaller schools have students who engage more frequently as actors in the life of the school. In a more recent study, Lindsay (1982) found that students in smaller high schools were more satisfied with their schools and attended class more regularly than did their counterparts in larger institutions.

At least two of the most eminent scholars in rural education have very specifically articulated what they claim are the pedagogical benefits of smallness. Faith Dunne (1977) points out that small classrooms with extensive community support and high teacher expectations and rapport have always been called for in the national literature on school reform. However, while her studies have found such attributes to be typical in rural schools, school administrators bent on consolidation during the past several decades have conveniently overlooked theses "pluses" in their efforts to centralize school curricula and staffing patterns. Bruce Barker (1986) has gone further than Dunne in arguing that many if not most of the new wave of proposed school reforms have been pioneered and proven in many rural schools in the U.S., despite the efforts of mainstream educational theory to abandon them throughout the years. In his overview of small schools literature, he argues that such schools are being rediscovered as models for effective schools, in terms of more individualized instruction, cross-age groupings, more supportive home-school relationships, peer tutoring, etc.

As this brief overview hopefully suggests, perhaps the major battleline in the rural school literature still forms around community control versus appropriate school size. Proponents of school consolidation and centralization have argued that many rural communities are too poor and/or too small to give their children adequate education. Supporters of local control argue that community life depends on the local school as a community resource, and with the proper funding formulas and decentralization, can be made viable both for community and individual academic achievement. In order to document the latter claim, alternative community-based strategies of school improvement not necessarily consistent with state mandated centralization and consolidation reforms have been very visible in the literature. For example, Paul Nachtigal's edited collection (1982) summarized over a dozen grassroots and foundation-sponsored attempts to save and enhance many rural school programs in the U.S. This reader in rural school innovation described how different citizen groups utilized experimental programs, national diffusion networks, leadership training strategies, and community building efforts via public education. And besides the Foxfire experience already mentioned, two other attempts to articulate how school and community life should be jointly enhanced were authored by Gjelten (1978) and Olsen (1954).

While most of the rural school advocates speak positively about the virtues of small town community life, there has also been some literature potentially unflattering to rural communities, particularly in Appalachia. In these states, school consolidation policies in economically disadvantaged districts have occasionally given rise to very powerful school superintendents, and they frequently have been charged with using school employment practices to enhance the status of their friends and relatives, rather than to improve educational opportunities for district children (Ogletree, 1977; Sher, 1983; Shrag, 1966). As well, it is typically among disadvantaged rural populations where objections to "secular humanism" as taught by "outsiders" with "blasphemous" textbooks have also been at least partially successful (Cummings, et. al., 1977; Page and Clelland, 1978). According to such sources, disputes between local and state constituents over rural educational policies focus not only on administrative issues, but also on a set of complex curricular questions, where teachers may be seen to represent a relatively cosmopolitan outside world juxtaposed against other community leaders whose status and authority lie in more conservative religious and traditional habits.

Comprehensive Efforts to Construct an Educational Research Agenda

Given that more objective educational research and scholarship on rural education is in essence less than a decade old, it should be no surprise that available works in this area are relatively obscure, lacking in focus, and relatively unsophisticated by contemporary standards. And this phenomenon has led to several interesting discussions of what we do and don't know about rural schools, each typically also containing proposals for remedying the situation (e.g., Stevens 1985) Many have argued that an essential first step in understanding the status of rural schooling lies in better empirical data bases to help researchers and policy makers get some working notions of the nature of rural education. In addition to the historical oversight of rural schools in the U.S., another major stumbling block to understanding their operations seems to be their great diversity. According to Helge (1985):

> The diversity of rural school subcultures is significant. For example, the geographic range includes remote islands and deserts as well as small clustered communities; an economic range from stable classic farm communities to depressed lower socioeconomic settings and high growth "boom or bust" communities; and a range of population sparsity from one-room school districts to schools located in small clustered towns or surrounded by other small districts. (p.1-2)

One of the main problems in discussions of rural school research and policy involves a lack of consensus about appropriate definitions of rural education. For example, the National School Board Association defines a district as rural if:

> it is located in a rural setting, or the student enrollment is 2,500 or less, or it's an intermediate or county unit that serves primarily rural units, or it encounters problems related to areas with population density of fewer than 1000 (residents) per square mile.

On the other hand, the National Rural Development Institute defines a rural district as one where:

> ...the number of inhabitants is less than 150 per square mile or when located in counties with 60% of the population living in communities no larger than 5000 inhabitants. Districts with more than 10,000 students and/or in (SMSA's) as defined by the Census are not considered rural.

Several ambitious studies have been mounted during the past five years in an effort to establish some baseline data on the form and functioning of rural and small schools (Dunne and Carlsen, 1981; Helge, 1985; Hubel and Barker, 1986; Rosenfeld, 1981). Purposes of these comprehensive surveys were all directed at looking for common themes as articulated by various school personnel which might be used to construct rural education research and policy agendas, given earlier oversight and the geographical and financial differences between many rural school districts. Importantly, there seemed some consensus about these themes across the studies.

Perhaps the best of these surveys was the one completed by Dunne and Carlsen, in that its focus was upon the perceived strengths and weaknesses of rural education around the country as reported by over one thousand teachers, administrators and school board members. Their final report also included eight case studies of small and rural schools in various parts of the country. In general, this study did find that many small and rural schools were strongly supported by their local communities, even more so than the national average. As well, three of the four greatest problems identified with public education around the nation were viewed as non-problematic by respondents in the Dunne and Carlsen study, emphasizing once again the distinctiveness of the rural and small school experience in the U.S. On the other hand, their research did suggest that many small schools continuously wrestle with some of the staffing and financing themes expressed in virtually all of the other comprehensive looks at problems of contemporary rural education in America.

Education and Rural Development

Just as in national assessments of student performance, economic disadvantage has been found to be systematically related to student underachievement in rural America, and especially in Appalachia (Weaver, 1977; DeYoung, 1985b). However, an interesting theme in much of the domestic and international rural education literature is a systematic discussion of the role of rural schools in vocational training and stimulating and/or enhancing local economic growth. Both of these topics have historically been seen in this literature, with the latter of even more concern in recent work. One reason this appears to be the case seems to reside in the post-high school opportunities of rural youth, many of whom do not go on to college and instead have traditionally sought vocational programs either in their high schools or in regional vocational education centers. Interestingly, many of the most widely recognized names in the scholarship on rural education have been particularly interested in this area. Hobbs (1979), for example, has described how successful rural schools were in the early twentieth century in terms of exporting skilled labor to urban areas for their development. At the same time, he argues, educational programs useful to America's farmers helped them usher in the age of mechanized farming upon which modernization has depended. As Fratoe (1979) points out, state and federal governments have been particularly active agents in rural education during the twentieth century by sponsoring three types of training programs relevant to rural development. These include(d): career and vocational programs sponsored by the Office of Education, several types of CETA programs targeted for various unemployed minority populations in rural areas, and various school extension programs (like 4H) designed to focus on topics like agriculture and home economics frequently not part of the public school curriculum.

Rosenfeld (1983) and Sher (1977), on the other hand, have been particularly interested in the decline of rural economies during the past decade, and have proposed new ways of trying to link public education to economic development. Rosenfeld, for example, argues that the two primary thrusts of occupational training during the past three decades currently have little utility in rural America. No longer, he suggests, can either vocational agriculture programs or industrial education efforts be productive in the countryside, because mechanization has replaced most agricultural opportunities in rural America, and the textile, apparel, and metal fabrication industries are increasingly leaving this country for overseas locations. Both Rosenfeld and Sher argue that the public school needs to become a site with specific economic development interests, in that the public school curriculum and/or its extracurricular focus should be on fostering local small business development projects in partnership with local business or independently. While noting the possible political difficulties of achieving such programs in some rural communities, they also point out successful examples, such as Wigginton's various Foxfire enterprises.

Conclusion

Most if not all of the scholars who work in the area of rural and small schools tend to agree on several perspectives of the field. They all tend to agree, for example, that rural education in America has been a stepchild to other aims and interests of professional educators and researchers alike. Importantly, they also typically claim that administrative, curricular, and staffing solutions to educational problems in metropolitan America may or may not have utility for rural education. The demographic, economic, administrative, vocational and community differences and needs existing in many rural regions of the country, it is argued, demand more particular attention by educational researchers and policy makers if rural schools are ever to achieve their full potential.

Educational research on rural and small schools has been minimal and marginal, it has been argued, for several reasons. Historically, the hope and expectation among educational professionals was that the demise of rural America and its schools was inevitable for a modern America. Subsequently, it was assumed that advances in curriculum and instruction based on social and administrative science would lead to one best system of benefit to all American schools. And when full-blown educational research and development efforts became important during the past thirty years, funded research primarily focused on problems of urban school districts in the U.S.

Currently, the consensus among growing numbers of educational researchers and policy makers is that rural education deserves more particular attention than it has historically received. This is necessary, they claim, because we now know that rural areas of the country have different and divergent needs; that past state and federal mandates have hindered as well as helped improvement of rural schools; and because local, state and federal governments are increasingly seeking to upgrade rural schools in efforts to attract and promote economic development.

For their part, educational researchers have begun to call for more and more sophisticated research on the particular issues and needs of rural schools. Noting that rural communities frequently find their schools more satisfactory than do metropolitan ones, and observing that smallness may facilitate rather than inhibit educational excellence, there seems to be renewed interest in the possibilities of rural and small schools as educational models. This renewed interest, if not expertise, is clearly documented in the increasing number of published articles on rural education in mainstream educational journals and the emergence of at least three new journals specifically related to rural education, including *Research in Rural Education, The Journal of Small and Rural Schools, and The Rural Educator*. As well, many states now have their own clearinghouses on rural education and research, joined recently by the federally funded Clearinghouse on Rural Education and Small Schools, located in Las Cruces, New Mexico, at New Mexico State University.

With particular regard to the historical and future development of meaningful educational policy in Appalachia, however, it could be argued that the situation is more problematic than on the national level. Having been identified early as a backward area, much of Appalachian public schooling was the target of various reforms from outside the region (DeYoung and Boyd, 1986; Silver and DeYoung, 1985). And even the most prestigious and respected private schools in Appalachia have been "fotched on". Most settlement schools and later college programs were typically operated by outsiders dedicated either to importing liberal arts education or to developing folk schools whose pedagogical and curricular forms originated elsewhere (Whisnant, 1983).

More recent efforts to "improve" Appalachian schools have typically pitted national compensatory education programs against the vested interests of local school superintendents. Forced to choose between accepting federal programs designed to improve supposedly inferior childrearing techniques of Appalachia's poor and/or accepting the inevitability of the educational status quo within an educational arena governed by the politics of school hiring suggests a less than desirable future for many Appalachian communities. And if current educational reform efforts further remove compensatory and entitlement programs for the schools and replace local politicians with state ones, how local communities will benefit is still unclear. The rhetoric notwithstanding, current educational reforms dedicated to the raising of test scores and attendance rates is tied to state and national educational investment strategies rather than to local community needs or issues.

If there is any hope of redressing urban-oriented school history and reform in Appalachia, it probably resides with the potential success of current grassroots movements linking rural education and community development to the rural farm crisis in this country, and/or to other regional study and policy interested groups which attempt to frame issues like education in political terms. Just like activists in Appalachian studies who are concerned about the politics of land ownership, water quality and health, the politics of education and the politics of school reform will have to be identified more visibly as issues in Appalachia in the future. "Where we are going" in Appalachian education depends upon the role local communities play in the future. Lack of attention, or depending on the insights of professionals and/or state and federal politicians, will probably give us more of the same. I hope this is not the path that will be followed.

A more complete overview of the status of American rural education scholarship is available in the authors article entitled "The Status of American Rural Education Research: An Integrated Review and Commentary," which is forthcoming in *Review of Educational Research*.

REFERENCES

Barker, B. (1986). *The Advantages of Small Schools*. Las Cruces, New Mexico: ERIC Clearinghouse on Rural Education and Small Schools. ERIC doc. ED 265988.

Barker, B. & Muse, I. (1983). *Research findings on K-12 and 1-12 Rural School Districts in the United States*. Paper presented at the annual meeting of the Rural Education Association. Manhatten, Kansas, Oct 16-18. Eric doc. ED 234973.

Barker, R. & Gump, P., (1964). *Big School, Small School*. Stanford, Ca.: Stanford University Press.

Barnhardt, R. (1977). *Cross-Cultural Issues in Alaskan Education*. Fairbanks, Alaska: Center for Northern Educational Research.

Barnhardt, R. (1982). *Cross-Cultural Issues in Alaskan Education* (vol. 2). Fairbanks, Alaska: Center for Northern Educational Research.

Beale, C. (1975). *The Revival of Growth in Nonmetropolitan America*. Washington, D.C.: U.S. Government Printing Office

Butler, R., and Monk, D. (1985). The cost of public schooling in New York State: the role of scale and efficiency in 1978-1979. *Journal of Human Resources*, 20(3), 361-381.

Callahan, R. (1962) *Education and the Cult of Efficiency*. Chicago: Univ. of Chicago Press.

Coles, R. (1967). *Children of Crisis (vol. 1): A Study of Courage and Fear*. New York: Dell.

Coles, R. (1970). *Uprooted Children: The Early Life of Migrant Farmworkers.* Pittsburg, PA.: University of Pittsburgh Press.

Coles, R. (1972). *Children of Crisis (vol.2): Migrants, Sharecroppers and Mountaineers.* Boston: Little Brown.

Conant, J. (1959). *The American High School Today.* New York: McGraw-Hill.

Conroy, P. (1972). *The Water is Wide.* Boston: Houghton Miffli Cooper, S. and Fitzwater, C. (1954). *County School Administration.* New York: Harper and Row.

Cubberley, E. (1914). *Rural Life and Education: A Study of the Rural School Problem as a Phase of the Rural Life Problem.* New York: Houghton Mifflin

Cummings, S., Briggs, R., & Mercy, J. (1977). Preachers versus teachers: local-cosmopolitan conflict over textbook censorship in an Appalachian community. *Rural Sociology,* 42 (1), 7-21.

Darnell, F. & Simpson, P. (1981). *Rural Education: In Pursuit of Excellence.* Nedlands, Western Australia: National Center for Research on Rural Education.

De La Garza, C. (1979). *Equity for Migrant Children in Rural Areas.* Washington, D.C.: National Institute on Education. ERIC doc. ED 172983.

Dennison, G. (1969). The Lives of Children: The Story of the First Street School. New York: Random House. DeYoung, A. (1985a). Inequality in school revenues: comparing school district expenditures and income sources in four rural states. *Journal of Educational Equity and Leadership,* 5(2), 107-118.

DeYoung, A. (1985b). Economic development and educational status in Appalachian Kentucky. *Comparative Education Review,* 29(1), 47-67.

DeYoung, A. & Boyd, T. (1987). Urban school reforms for a rural district: a case study of school/community relations in Jackson County Kentucky, 1899 - 1986. *Journal of Thought,* 21:4 (Winter) 25-42.

Dunne, F. (1977). Choosing smallness: an examination of the small school experience in rural America. in Sher, J. *Education in Rural America.*

Dunne, F. & Carlson, W. (1981). *Small Rural Schools in the United States: A Statistical Profile.* Washington D.C.: The National Rural Center.

Fratoe, F. (1978). *Rural Education and the Rural Labor Force in the Seventies.* Washington, D.C.: Economics, Statistics, and Cooperative Service, U.S. Department of Agriculture, Rural Research Report 5.

Fratoe, F. (1979). *Education Training Programs and Rural Development.* Washington, D.C.: National Institute of Education. ERIC doc. ED172967.

Fuller, W. (1982). *The Old Country School: The Story of Rural Education in the Middle West.* Chicago: Univ. of Chicago Press.

Gjelten, T. (1978). *Schooling in Isolated Communities.* Portland, Maine: North Haven Project.

Goodlad, J. (1984). *A Place Called School*. New York: McGraw-Hill.

Grantham, D. (1983). *Southern Progressivism: The Reconciliation of Progress and Tradition*. Knoxville: Univ. of Tennessee Press.

Greenwood, K. (1982). An historical look at politics in vocational education. *Politics of Vocational Education*. Arlington Virginia: American Vocational Association, pp. 3-19.

Guthrie, J. (1979). Organizational scale and school success. *Educational Evaluation and Policy Analysis*, 1(1), 17-27.

Harrington, M. (1962). *The Other America: Poverty in the United States*. Baltimore, Md.: Penguin Books.

Heath, S. B., (1983). *Ways With Words: Language, Life, and Work in Communities and Classrooms.D Cambridge, England: Cambridge University Press*

Hecht, K. (1981). The educational challenge in rural Alaska: era of local control. In Sher, J. (ed.) *Rural Education in Urbanized Nations: Issues and Innovations*.Helge, D. (1981). Problems in implementing comprehensive special education programming in rural areas. *Exceptional Children*, 50(4) 294-305.

Helge, D. (1985). *Establishing a National Rural Education Research Agenda*. Bellingham, Wa: National Rural Development Institute.

Herndon, J. (1968). *The Way it Spozed to Be*. New York: Simon and Schuster, Inc.

Hirsch, M. (1928). An experimental study of the East Kentucky mountaineers. *Genetic Psychology Monographs*, 3(3), 189-244.

Hobbs, D. (1979). *Education in Rural America: Object or Instrumentality of Rural Development*. Washington, D.C.: National Institute of Education. LKIL doc. [0 172966.

Horn, J. (1983). Attempting to develop a program response to the needs of those preparing to teach in rural/small schools. Paper presented at the AERA Annual Meeting, Montreal, Quebec, Canada.

Horn, J. (1985). *Recruitment and Preparation of Quality Teachers Rural Schools*. Washington, D.C.: U.S. Department of Education.

Horn, J., Davis, P., & Hilt, R. (1985). Importance of areas of preparation for teaching in rural/small schools. *Research in Rural Education* 3(1), 23-29.

Hubel, K., & Barker, B. (1986). *Rural Education Association Research Agenda Report*. Fort Collins, Colorado: Colorado State University.

Huebner, E., Cummings, J., & McLesky, J. (1985). The delivery of quality assessment services to rural handicapped children. *Research in Rural Education* 2(4), 151-154.

Huebner, E. & Huberty, T, (1984). Burnout among rural school psychologists. *Research in Rural Education*, 2(3), 95-99.

Katz, M. (1977). From voluntarism to bureaucracy in American education in J. Karabel and Halsey, A. (eds.) *Power and Ideology in Education*, 383-397.

Key, C. (1932). The intelligence of isolated mountain children. *Child Development*, 3(4), 279-290.

Kleinfeld, J. (1972). *Effective Teachers of Indian and Eskimo High School Students*. Fairbanks, Alaska: Center for Northern Educational Research and Institute of Social, Economic and Government Research.

Kohl, H. (1967). *36 Children*. New York: New American Library, Inc.

Kozol, J. (1967). Death at an Early Age. New York: Houghton Mifflin Co.

Lindsay, P. (1982). The effect of high school size on student participation, satisfaction and attendance. *Educational Evaluation and Policy Analysis* (Spring)...

Looff, D. (1971). *Appalachia's Children*. Lexington, Ky.: University Press of Kentucky.
Lynd, R. & Lynd, H. (1937). *Middletown in Transition*. New York: Harcourt, Brace and World.

Massey, S. & Crosby, J. (1983). Special problems, special opportunities: preparing teachers for rural schools. *Phi Delta Kappan*, 65(4) 265-269.

Mathes, W. & Carlson, R. (1986). Conditions for practice: why teachers select rural schools. *Journal of Rural and Small Schools* 1(1), 25-28.

McLeskey, J., Cummings, J., Huebner, E. & Waldron, N. (1983). An administrative perspective on psychological services in rural school settings. *Research in Rural Education*, 2(2), 85-88.

Muse, I. (1977). Preservice programs for educational personnel going into rural schools. Washington: D.C. National Institute of Education ERIC doc. ED 135506.

Nachtigal, P. (1980). *Improving Rural Schools*. Washington: National Institute of Education. ERIC Doc. td 192922.

Nachtigal, P. (1982). *Rural Education: In Search of a Better Way*. Boulder, Colorado: Westview Press.

National Center for Educational Statistics (1980). *Statistics of Local Public School Systems*. Washington, D.C.: U.S. Government Printing Office.

Ogletree, J. (1977). Appalachian schools - a case of consistency. In Mielke, D. (ed.) Teaching Mountain Children. Boone, N.C.: Appalachian Consortium Press, 184-197.

Olsen, E. (1954). *School and Community*. New York: Prentice Hall.

Page, A. & Clelland, D. (1978). The Kanawha County textbook controversy: a study in the politics of lifestyle concern. *Social Forces* 57(1) 265-281.

Perkinson, H. (1968). *The Imperfect Panacea: American Faith in Education, 1865-1976*. New York: Random House.

Peshkin, A. (1978). *Growing Up American: Schooling and the Survival of Community*. Chicago: Univ. of Chicago Press.

Peshkin, A. (1982). *The Imperfect Union: School Consolidation and Community Conflict*. Chicago: Univ. of Chicago Press.Precourt, W. (1982). Ethnohistorical analysis of an Appalachian settlement school. In G. Spindler (ed.) *Doing the Ethnography of Schooling*. New York: Holt, Rinehart and Winston.

Puckett, J. (1986). Foxfire Reconsidered: A Critical Ethnohistory of a Twenty-Year Experiment in Progressive Education. Unpublished Doctoral Dissertation, University of North Carolina.

Ravitch, D. (1983). *The Troubled Crusade*. New York: Basic Books.

Reed, D. & Busby, D. (1985). Teacher incentives in rural schools. Research in *Rural Education* 3(2), 69-73.

Rosenfeld, S. (1977). Centralization versus decentralization: a case study of rural education in Vermont. in Sher (ed.) *Education in Rural America*, 205-270.

Rosenfeld, S. (1981). *A Portrait of Rural America: Conditions Affecting Vocational Education Policy*. Washington, D.C.: U.S. Department of Education

Rosenfeld, S. (1983). Something old, something new: the wedding of rural education and rural development. *Phi Delta Kappan* 65(4), 270-273.

Rosenfeld, S. & Sher, J. (1977). The urbanization of rural schools. in Sher, J. (ed.) *Education in Rural America*, 11-42.

Sher, J. (1977). *Education in Rural America: A Reassessment of Conventional Wisdom*. Boulder, Colorado: Westview Press.

Sher, J. (1981). *Rural Education in Urbanized Nations: Issues and Innovations*. Boulder, Colorado: Westview Press.

Sher, J. (1983). Bringing home the bacon: the politics of rural school reform. *Phi Delta Kappan*, 65(4), 279-283.

Sher, J. & Tompkins, R. (1977). Economy, efficiency, and equality: the myths of rural school and district consolidation. In Sher, (ed.) *Education in Rural America*, 43-77.

Shrag, P. (1966). The school and politics. *Appalachian Review*, Fall, 6-10.

Silver, R. & DeYoung, A. (1985). The ideology of rural/appalachian education, 1895 - 1935: the appalachian education problem as part of the appalachian life problem. *Educational Theory*, 36 (1), 51 - 65.

Spindler, L. (1977). *Cultural Change and Modernization: Mini Models and Case Studies*. New York: Holt, Rinehart and Winston, Inc.

Stephens, E. (1985). Towards the construction of a research and development agenda for rural education. *Research In Rural Education*, 2(4), 167-171.

Tompkins, R. (1977). Coping with sparsity: a review of rural school finance. in Sher (ed.) *Education in Rural America*, 125-155.

Trenary, J. (1980). The unique problems of rural school psychologists. *The School Psychologist*, 23(4), 13.

Tyack, D. (1974). *The One Best System*. Cambridge, Mass: Harvard Univ. Press.

Tyack, D. & Hansot, E. (1982). *Managers of Virtue: Public School Leadership in America, 1820-1980*. New York: Basic Books.

Warner, W. & Lunt, P. (1941). *The Social Life of a Modern Community*. Vol. 1, "Yankee City Series". New Haven: Yale University Press.

Wax, M., Wax, R. & Dumont, R. (1964). Formal education in an American indian community. *Social Problems*, 2(4), 1-126.

Weaver, T. (1977). Class conflict in rural education: a case study of Preston County, West Virginia. In Sher, (ed.) *Education in Rural America*, 159-203.

Whisnant, D. (1983). *All That is Native and Fine*. Chapel Hill, N.C.: University of North Carolina Press.

Wigginton, E. (1985). *Sometimes a Shining Moment*. Garden City, New York: Anchor Press.

PARTNERING FOR RESEARCH
   Convenor: Howard Dorgan, Appalachian State University
Partnering with the Indigenous: Teaming With The Marshall Family to Study Old Regular Baptists
   Howard Dorgan, Appalachian State University
   Darvin Marshall, Coeburn, Virginia
   Ganell Marshall, Coeburn, Virginia

Partnering for Research in Appalachia

by
Howard Dorgan

I became acquainted with Darvin and Ganell Marshall in 1982. That year they provided me my first contact with Old Regular Baptists, an Appalachian religious faction staunchly preserving worship traditions dating from the eighteenth and nineteenth centuries. Prior to this work with the Marshalls, my own knowledge of Old Regulars had come from the film, "In the Good Old Fashioned Way,"[1] and from essays by Ron Short and John Wallhausser, "We Believe in the Family and the Old Regular Baptist Church" and "I Can Almost See Heaven From Here."[2] My own field research before the spring of 1982 had been with Missionary, Union, Primitive, Regular, and Free Will Baptists in the northwest corner of North Carolina.[3]

In April, 1982, I decided to devote the following summer to an examination of "Homecoming" traditions in the mountains of North Carolina. Preparatory for this project, I approached the news bureau at Appalachian State University to suggest a news release on my plans, one which would include an announcement that I wanted invitations to a number of these annual events.

The article was written, and it ran in several small newspapers and specialty publications of the region, including the *High Country Magazine*[4], a newsprint journal servicing the Southern Appalachian tourist trade. A copy of this article made its way to Florida where a sister of Darvin Marshall saw it. She in turn phoned Darvin at his home on Sandy Ridge, just north of Coeburn, Virginia. This serendipitous set of circumstances engendered a series of other actions that ultimately propelled me into a study of the Old Regular Baptists of Appalachia.

About the Marshalls and Sandy Ridge

Darvin and Ganell Marshall live on Virginia's Route 654, approximately two hundred yards from the Sandy Ridge Old Regular Baptist Church, the fellowship with which Darvin's late father had been affiliated. In 1982 Darvin and Ganell regularly attended the services of this church, although neither was then, or is now, a member of this or any other Old Regular fellowship. Nevertheless, over the years Darvin had developed a deep fondness for the small church and a profound love and respect for the "Old Time Way" traditions of this Baptist sect. He feels strongly that the customs, beliefs, and values of this faith should be documented, having inherited this attitude from his father who once helped a wandering scholar interested in Old Regular lined singing.[5]

One morning I was in my office at Appalachian State University when I received a call from Darvin. Would I like to visit some Old Regular Baptist churches, he asked. My answer was quick and in the affirmative.

Darvin immediately sent me the published minutes of the 1981 annual meeting of the Union Association of Old Regulars, and at the same time invited me to attend a service at the Sandy Ridge church. As it turned out, however, the first Old Regular fellowship I visited was Bethany in Kingsport, Tennessee. Information supplied in those '81 minutes enabled me to contact Elder Foster Mullins, assistant moderator of that congregation, with whom I arranged that first visit. Later I traveled to Sandy Ridge, witnessed a service at that church, met Elder Raymond Smith (then the moderator of the Sandy Ridge fellowship, and an individual who has become strongly supportive of my research), stayed for a fellowship meal in what was once a two-room schoolhouse, but which has become the Sandy Ridge Community Center, and established my acquaintance with Darvin and his family. Since that time, the Marshalls and I have traveled over much of the Central Appalachian Plateau, visiting numerous Old Regular churches, with Darvin serving as my guide and contact, and with Ganell providing assistance in understanding Old Regular women and the Old Regular home and family.

Sandy Ridge lies about seven miles due north of Coeburn, in Wise County. It is a beautiful area that so far displays—in any highly visible way—only minimal scarring from strip mining. The ugly cuts are there. In fact one particularly unattractive one exists about a mile below the Marshall's home. However, most of the stripped areas on this and surrounding ridges can be seen only if one gets off the main roads, and Appalachian nature is kind, quickly camouflaging many of the rude gashes. Still, the numerous harms of strip mining are felt on "The Ridge," not the least of which is the problem of altered water flows and acidic run-offs. The Marshall's own water has become partially contaminated as the result of stripping on the ridge above their house.

One of the best known residents of Sandy Ridge is Ralph Stanley, widely recognized for his Blue Grass picking and singing. With a late brother, this native musician recorded a number of albums of Appalachian folk tunes[6] and is now a frequent guest on such respected traditional music programs as "Austin City Limits."

Other residents of this ridge tend to be from a sturdy, yeoman farmer heritage, most of Scotch-Irish descent, and many representing families that have occupied this land for a number of generations. Marshalls, for example, have been in southwest Virginia since the late seventeen hundreds, initially possessing land granted for service in the Revolutionary War. Unfortunately many of the present occupants of the ridge inherited their holdings with the mineral rights already sold to coal companies, transactions that have victimized several generations of these ridge dwellers. A good portion of the present owners of this land now work for the coal companies, as miners, haulers, large machinery operators, etc.

Darvin Marshall spent his last working years in a bank in Coeburn, a job from which he took early retirement because of a major heart attack. Ganell has always been a housewife, but now she also works the craft fair business, selling corn-shuck dolls that she makes in the basement of her home. Both of the Marshalls possess a deep appreciation for their cultural heritage, and they have adopted Appalachian studies somewhat as a hobby. In the process they have also adopted my research. The result has been a partnership which has assisted my entrance into the semiclosed world of Old Regularism. This paper examines some obvious advantages of partnering with the indigenous for Old Regular research and focuses on the particular contributions of the Marshalls to this specific study.

Contributions of the Marshalls

The advantages of working with someone like the Marshalls in the study of Old Regulars are numerous, not the least of which is the fact that these churches are very difficult to locate without someone familiar with the region as your guide. Not only are the buildings often tucked away from main roads, but they are remarkably inconspicuous. Seldom will they have steeples or other architectural features, such as stained glass windows, to identify them clearly as houses of worship. In addition, the familiar church marquee, announcing a minister and schedule of services, is not a feature of Old Regular meeting houses. Furthermore, large signs are traditionally not characteristic of these churches, either down on the road or on the front of the building. There usually is a sign, but only a very modest one that announces the name of the church and the year it was founded. One result of all this is that a would-be visitor to an Old Regular church frequently has to park his or her car on the side of the road and walk right up in front of the respective meeting house before being certain of the building's identity.

Darvin and I have now located fifteen associations of Old Regular churches: New Salem (the mother of them all), Union (the second oldest, but first in total number of fellowships), Thornton Union, two Indian Bottom groups, two Mountain Associations, Sardis, Old Friendship, Friendship, Philadelphia, Northern New Salem, Mud River, Bethel, and Mountain Liberty (the most recently formed of the lot). There may be a sixteenth group, the Kyova Association, which once flourished in West Virginia; but neither Darvin or I have been able to establish that this cluster still exists, at least as true Old Regular fellowships. A seventeenth group, the Cumberland Association, once operated in the Wise County region of Virginia, but these churches abandoned[7] their affiliation with Old Regularism.

Darvin has mapped the general boundaries of eight of these associations and is making rapid progress in locating the individual churches within each of these clusters. This research is of course valuable to me, and its worth is increased several fold when Darvin is able to guide me through a maze of narrow mountain roads directly to a respective church. Early in my field work, I learned that it was no easy matter to find a particular meeting house simply by following directions given by the fellowship's moderator or clerk. Most researchers who have worked extensively with indigenous Appalachians realize that these people tend to give directions not by road numbers and highway signs, but by natural geographical features of the land-ridges, hollows, creeks, rivers, bottoms, forks, etc. I have often been amused at the close of Old Regular services when visiting elders give their "appointments," announcements during which the meeting Sundays of their home churches are given, along with directions to the respective houses of worship. What one usually hears are recitations of strings of geographical features, each appended to an identifying ablative (Caney Ridge, Turkey Creek, Cedar Bottom, Bent Branch, Rocky Fork), all followed by the apparently obligatory conclusion, "You can't miss it." Needless to say, I found that I could frequently "miss it," unless the Marshalls were showing the way or actually driving me to the spot.

Locating a church, however, is obviously just the first step: The researcher must meet the people, become accepted as a nonthreatening and friendly agent, and learn how to talk to the various elements in the fellowship. Again the Marshalls have often made the difference between success and failure, giving my work an aura of acceptability and providing information critical to determining viable strategies of approach. Wherever we go Darvin works the crowd before and after the service, speaking enthusiastically to church leaders about my study, selling the idea that Old Regularism must be documented. In addition, he collects information applicable to other visitations—types of services scheduled, location of churches, names of contact persons, and the like. In a very real sense, Darvin and Ganell have become participating partners in my research and must eventually share in any triumphs arising from it.

Ganell's role in all of this has centered on providing me a better understanding of the Old Regular woman and the Old Regular family. After one of my early presentations on gender roles in Old Regularism, Pat Beaver warned that I might never capture the true essence of the Old Regular woman without a female assistant who could relate to these matrons.[8] To a large degree, Ganell has become that assistant, helping me appreciate better the feminine point of view within Old Regularism. In particular, she has persistently warned me about moving toward stereotypes when discussing some of the restrictions placed upon the appearance and behavior of these women. I have had somewhat of a tendency to do that when examining restrictions concerning Old Regular women's hair, dress, participation in worship, and voice in church governance; but Ganell is always there to pull me back from generalizations that become too sweeping. It is just too easy for an outsider to see these Old Regular women solely in terms of their uncut hair, their emotional shouting in services, their modest dress styles, their voiceless position in church politics, their subservient or nonexistent role in liturgical functions, and their stand-back-and-wait attentiveness to males during after-service fellowship meals. The subtle ways in which they exert themselves in home, community, and church are more difficult to see and understand, but Ganell has frequently focused my attention on these less obvious female wieldings of power and influence.

Both Darvin and Ganell have read the notes I have written after each visitation and the several essays I have authored about Old Regulars, and their careful scrutinizations of these materials have provided a valuable check on any possible inaccuracies and misinterpretations. In this process they haven't tried to move me toward unrealistically positive attitudes, just as they haven't exposed me only to the more modern associations and fellowships.

Old Regular theology constitutes a particularly difficult area for total understanding, primarily because there is so little of the faith's doctrine that has been expressed in precise creedal form. Each association publishes its articles of faith in its annual minutes, but these statements are sketchy in character and leave wide areas for interpretation. There is no Old Regular document that delineates the faith theology in as complete an exposition, for example, as the Philadelphia Confession did for eighteenth century Regular Baptists, and many Old Regular elders struggle as much in expressing the sect's precise beliefs as do outsiders. An individual article of faith becomes clearer, however, when one understands the historical environments in which it was forged, including the countermovement to which it was a response. Therefore, during evenings spent in the Marshalls' home, Darvin and I have wandered widely over both the historical and theological developments of Old Regularism. Doctrinal understandings gained during these sessions have later been tested in discussions with such Old Regular leaders as Elder Edwin May, Moderator of the Sardis Association.[9]

During theological discussions Ganell stands to the side, saying that the exposition of doctrine is Darvin's "gift." However, I think I see in her actions in this regard simply a deference to the traditional male role in debating doctrinal matters. Still, Darvin does know his Bible, and is usually able to identify the scripture used in justification of Old Regular theology.

The Marshalls not only have helped me in knowing about Old Regulars, but they also have contributed heavily to my understanding of the entire cultural and geographical environment within which Old Regularism exists. The long drives from Sandy Ridge to churches in Kentucky or other areas of Virginia have provided opportunity for discussions of mining in Appalachia; the ethnography of the people; the nomenclature of ridges, creeks, and bottoms; politics of coal; education in the mountains; identification of Appalachian values; and a host of similar topics. In addition, these hours of travel have often been spent in examinations of the Appalachian image, with both Darvin and Ganell expressing their concerns for the stereotypes generally associated with this image. They enjoy speaking against the tendency in mass media—and in some Appalachian scholarship—to concentrate on the bleak scenes of economic decay in the old mining camps, the suggestions of cultural and educational backwardness, the Hatfield and McCoy depictions of social mores, the Deliverance images of Appalachian character, and the "snakehandling-is-the-mode" generalizations about Appalachian religious traditions. Concerns such as these no doubt stand behind Ganell's insistence that I look beyond the surface eccentricities of Old Regularism (women not being allowed to cut their hair) to the deeper values and precepts of the faith. Darvin, on the other hand, hopes I will see beauty, virtue, and strength of character in the denomination's tenacious preservations of customs and beliefs, history wed to a spiritual mission.

Concluding Observations

I might have been able to establish contact with Old Regularism without the assistance of Darvin and Ganell, but I would have been forced to move more slowly than I have been able to do as a result of their help. In addition, I am certain that I would not have felt as confident in my analyses had I not formed this partnership for research. Therefore, I view this linking with the Marshalls as having been an essential element of any success experienced in this project.

There are dangers in such methods: Scholarly objectivity could become subverted by friendships, conclusions that might offend could be avoided, exposure to the phenomenon being studied could become highly selective, and general emotional contact with subject matter could become intensified. These are problems faced by every student of humanity and human institutions, since we form bonds so quickly; but this same closeness and empathic identification can endow the investigator with special sensitivities needed for total understanding. My partnership with the Marshalls has, by my perception, certainly aided my search for understanding

ENDNOTES

1. Appalshop Films, Whitesburg, Kentucky, 1973.

2. *Southern Exposure*, IV (No. 3), 60-65; *Katallasete*, (Spring1983), 2-10.

3. *See Howard Dorgan, Giving Glory to God in Appalachia: Worship Practices of Six Baptist Sub-denominations* (Knoxville, Tenn.: University of Tennessee Press, 1987).

4. "Homecoming," *High Country Magazine*, April 21, 1982.

5. I received this story from Darvin Marshall, but I have no details concerning the event.

6. "The Stanley Brothers of Virginia," Vols. I-IV (Floyd,Virginia: Produced by Country Records, 1976).

7. The Cumberland Association once corresponded with the Mountain Liberty Association, *Minutes* of the Mountain Liberty Association, 1973 (Published by the Association, 1973), 5.

8. After a presentation on Old Regular gender roles, presented at the Women's Studies Sandwich Seminar, Appalachian State University, 1986.

9. Interview, Abingdon, Virginia, Feb. 15, 1985.

REEVALUATING WOMEN'S ROLES
Convenor: Malinda Crutchfield, Appalachian Consortium
From: "Fotched-On" Women To The New Feminism: A Review of Women in Social Service Delivery for Women in Appalachia
Karen Tice, Western Carolina University
Albie Pabon, Western Carolina University
Gender and Class: The Social Reality of Low Income Appalachian Mothers
Judith Ivy Fiene, University of Tennessee
Coalmining Women In Appalachia
Carolyn Doyle, Radford University
Can The Means Make The Ends Meet? The Personal Context Of Work In The Lives Of Watauga County Craftswomen
Deborah J. Thompson, Appalachian State University
Polarities and Consciousness: The Distinctive Class/Gender Consciousness of Appalachian Coalminers and Their Wives
Michael Yarrow, Ithaca College
Ruth Yarrow, Beckley, West Virginia

From "Fotched-on Women" to the New Feminist Practice: Women and Social Work in Appalachia

by
Karen W. Tice and Albie Pabon

"*To live among people in a model home, to show them by example the advantages of cleanness, neatness, and order, and to inspire them to use pure language and lead pure Christian lives will be our effort, hoping thereby to elevate and uplift them.*" Settlement House Worker, 1901 (quoted in Whisnant, 1983:29).

"*You are really just pioneering in this thing. That's what keeps me going.*" Director of a Battered Woman's Program in Appalachia, 1987.

Historically, women were a major force in the early social uplift enterprises in Appalachia. Today, they continue their catalytic roles in challenging community and family norms in the region. This paper will examine continuities and change in the experiences of women social activists in Appalachia. Attention will be given to comparison between women's involvement in the early settlement house movement and women involved in today's efforts around issues involving battered women and rape. Whether the ideological underpinnings of these mobilization efforts, past and present, have been conservative or progressive has been a matter of considerable debate.

In his study of the politics of culture in Appalachia, *All That is Native and Fine*, David Whisnant has extensively critiqued the work of women in early uplift efforts, whom he terms the "fotched-on women," e.g., women from outside Appalachia who were motivated by cultural and revivalistic values to uplift the mountain people. He characterizes women settlement school leaders such as Katherine Petit and May Stone as agents of modernization who imported mass "culture" to the mountains in the form of manners, dress, eating habits, home decoration, and breeding (Whisnant, 1983:45). Surely the South during the period 1870 to 1930 was no progressive paradise for activist women. Yet Whisnant downplays the significant challenges that movement women of this era raised to traditional conceptions of women's sphere. With morality as the initial root and continued impetus for their social change efforts, women succeeded in broadening women's participation in community life in the rural mountains by their involvement in settlement schools, missionary societies, and the Women's Christian Temperance Union. Participation in such organizations provided a forum for training women as organizers and for legitimating women's activism in shaping society. Although limited in political vision by their class positions and by a hostile environment and rigid in perpetuating a constricted definition of women's proper role, "fotched-on women," nonetheless, provided a legacy and history for today's rural women activists in Appalachia.

In the name of God, family, temperance, literature, health, and tradition, women set out in large numbers to expand their housekeeping role for the inner sanctum of the home to the community. With their beginnings in missionary societies, in groups such as the W.C.T.U. with 800,000 members and the general federation of women's clubs with one million members, in settlement houses and schools, and in suffrage societies, women's visibility and social consciousness were intensified. Their range of issues, strategies, and philosophies was diverse, often in response to the local climate in which mobilization was occurring.

Women contributed to the development of Sunday schools, initiated prison reforms, child labor reforms, sanitation improvements, compulsory education, and struggled to reduce adult illiteracy. Under the protective canopy of spreading the social gospel and protecting the Christian middle class home, women learned many of the essential organizing skills from lobbying to recruitment that helped to loosen the confining shackles of traditional conceptions of southern womanhood. As Sallie Sims Cotten, a leader in the North Carolina women's club movement summed up, "the new force in modern civilization is educated, Christianized, organized womanhood" (quoted in Scott, 1984:164).

Unlike the work of their urban counterparts, much of the early efforts of women in North Carolina, Tennessee, and Kentucky concentrated on establishing craft-oriented industries such as Mrs. Vanderbilt's craft sales cooperative in Asheville and Frances Goodrich's craft cooperative, also in North Carolina. Along with cooking instruction, sewing lessons, the importance of washing and putting away the dishes, and music classes, an awareness of the larger ravages of rapid industrialization was sowed. As Alice Kessler-Harris (1981:115) points out, "settlement workers out of necessity turned from demonstrating virtue to actively participating in social and political life."

She observes that "to remedy poverty, activist women had to deal with unemployment; to promote cleanliness they had to confront discriminatory plans for sewage conditions that sapped energy and destroyed morale" (p. 115). A comment by Frances Willard, leader of the W.C.T.U., in a speech in Atlanta in 1890 reveals the radical potential such reform efforts implied. Acknowledging that labor unions were the hope of the future and urging upon industry a consideration of profit sharing, Willard said, "If this is to teach socialism, then let it be so" (quoted in Scott, 1984:208). Similarly, the president of the Tennessee League of Women Voters remarked that "some good souls are pleased to call our ideas socialistic, yet every clear thinking, right feeling, and high minded man and woman should consecrate his best talents to the gradual reorganization of society, national and international" (quoted in Scott, 227). In North Carolina, women were demanding a survey of the working conditions of women in the textile mills. As Scott (p. 205) sums up, "Even the fragmentary evidence here ... is enough to make clear that women had their own voice, though possibly its tone concealed its substance."

Whisnant's critique of the role of "fotched-on" women in Appalachia primarily consists of their avoidance of the issue of the class inequities of industrialization in the southern mountains. Instead, they artificially laid on a definition of social change as a matter of niceties, manners, morals, or a "politics of politeness." As Whisnant states, "Culture (as the women defined it in limited and romantic terms) became a diversion, a substitute for engaging with political and economic forces, processes, and institutions that were altering the entire basis of individual identity and social organization in the mountains" (p. 15). He adds that "Thus to this day there are a thousand people who know that mountaineers weave coverlets and sing ballads for every one who knows that millions of them have been industrial workers and have organized unions and picketed the state and national capitals" (p. 13).

Yet to so reduce women's work in the settlement schools, the W.C.T.U., and women's clubs as "depoliticized not just in content but in method of reform" (Whisnant, p. 15), is to ignore the complexities of women's movement work as well as the constraints imposed by rigid gender roles. As Kessler-Harris (p. 114) points out in the case of the W.C.T.U., "the sense of collective feminine values as an active force for achieving social change cannot be minimized." Additionally, the legitimation of women's active participation in shaping community and social life was assured. As the W.C.T.U. proclaimed, "women will bless and brighten every place she enters and she will enter every place" (quoted in Kessler-Harris, p. 113). Such early activities not only provided outlets for women to use their voices, learn organizing skills, extend values of the home into the world of men but also served as a diving board for women to plunge into struggles for social and economic justice.

Today, the work of battered women advocates in Appalachia continues the legacy of confronting the social order, often hampered as their historical counterparts were by the established order, along with new tightrope balancing acts required by professionalization pressures, lack of funding, and community defensiveness.

Roots of the Battered Women's Movement

The battered women's movement developed in a social climate filled with self-help projects, feminist organizing, and challenges to the idea that chastisement was needed to keep women in line. The feminist movement provided a platform and an atmosphere for asking questions about women's rights to control their bodies and lives without self-blame. The feminist movement provided the impetus for alerting social consciousness to gender oppression and provided an opportunity for women to gain organizing skills useful for establishing programs for battered women. The first shelters in the United States were established in large metropolitan areas, drawing upon the energy and expertise of feminist-based networks. "In St. Paul, Minnesota in 1971, one of the earliest shelters in the United States, Women Advocates, grew out of a consciousness-raising group" (Schechter, 1982:33). "Transition House in Cambridge, Massachusetts was started by two former battered women and two former members of Cell 16, one of Boston's early radical feminist groups" (Schechter, p. 34). These early prototypes would serve as blueprints for later programs and many of their innovations in structure, content, and analysis would shape the tone, style, and practice of later programs. Their spirit of innovation and an ongoing process of defining and specifying feminist praxis continue today.

A multiplicity of ideologies characterized the early movement organizers in their explanations of the oppression and subordination of women and in their solutions to violence against women. Many believed that equality could be achieved with men by reforming existing institutions and systems. More radical feminists saw battering as stemming from unequal power relations within the home and believed that only through profound transformations in the political and social arena would violence against women end (Schechter, pp. 45-51).

Feminist practice tenets often included an emphasis on consensual decision-making rather than upon voting, a commitment to politicizing the personal, and the importance of women's culture for political change and struggle. Many battered women's organizations felt that it was paramount to preserve an autonomous women's space, separate from male control and influence. Location of the program, however, became an important determinant of program politics as the movement spread. In more rural and conservative communities, feminism was synonymous with "home-breakers," lesbians, and subversives undermining the American Way. Often, there were fewer allies to choose from pre-established feminist groups; consequently, modification of more urban-based feminist politics occurred.

After 1976, hundreds of programs were established with CETA funds as well as with volunteer resources. Many strains erupted as programs faced numerous pressures and dilemmas and struggled to uphold vague vestiges of feminist praxis. They addressed many questions. How to gain funding without extolling a tax on autonomy? How strong a commitment should be made to hiring formerly battered women? How important are professional credentials for staff? How strongly must programs adhere to a commitment to a social change model as opposed to a mental health frame of reference? How do organizations cope with the daily pressures caused by problems of financial survival? What roles should advisory and governing boards play and who should be represented on these boards? How do organizations develop consistent politics while responding to crisis calls and dealing with local power structures? How do feminist and egalitarian values relate to status and salary matters? How committed to racial and ethnic diversity among staffmembers should a program be? How do programs gain and how far do they go to win community legitimacy? How do they deal with competition among programs for limited resources? Is there allegiance to a model of staff as helpers and experts and to battered women as clients? Is battering to be explained by a family pathology model or one that stresses the oppression of women? Is the clinical terminology "family violence" or the feminist terminology "battered women" to be the organization's calling card? What process and structure best support movement goals? These questions still reflect the growing pains and on-going struggles of today's organizations.

Flexibility has been and will continue to be essential for the survival of women's organizations. Many programs have had to recontextualize program politics to convince skeptical communities of the need for their services. Women's Advocates was asked to change its name to something less inflammatory (Schechter, p. 63). In rural areas, especially, the need to become embedded within the community fabric has necessitated new protective strategies. For what works in New York City, Boston, and Chicago cannot be imported directly to the rural southern mountains. Thus some of the problems which confronted early southern women activists and "fotched-on" women can be discerned in today's Appalachian battered women's advocates.

In order to explore the dynamics of region and locale on the structure and politics of women activist organizations, we have interviewed workers in four battered women's programs in four different rural Appalachian communities.

Battered-Women's Programs in Appalachia Today

In 1978, at the zenith of the development of movement based programs, a three-county joint effort was initiated to establish a "place where physically abused women could hide" in one rural section of the Appalachian mountain region. Two of the current programs we interviewed re-emerged in 1984 and 1985 out of this initial effort. A post-mortem analysis of this original effort, conducted by one of the early program organizers, highlights many of the tensions and strains that programs continue to confront today in rural Appalachia.

The initial organizing effort was conducted by professional social service providers described as "a board of women dedicated to a philosophy that the program would not have the normal hierarchical structure nor would it be run like men" would run it. Leadership was suspect and it was subtly discouraged. The board utilized a collaborative management model; decision-making was by consensus. A "coordinator" was hired and "she was the glue that held it all together." The coordinator later left because of board troubles. When a president of the board became the new coordinator, old and new tensions flared. The relationship between the board and staff continued to be at the root of problems. According to the post-mortem analyst, "It was like hiring your employer and telling him what to do." Men were brought onto the board for leadership purposes. Other strains noted in the report included the observation that battered women were resistant to asking for help from professionals, and were intimidated by "helpers who don't sound like us." The report also notes that "volunteers were outsiders and transients who didn't know what was going on here. There is sometimes an ethnocentric desire to raise the locals up to our standards."

Ambivalent feelings about power and authority, inadequate models for women's roles within the organization, blurred areas of responsibility, paranoia of strong leadership, lack of job descriptions, consensus decision-making as an inefficient method taking too much time and energy, county rivalries, and funding crises were all perceived as eroding feelings of success and leading to insecurity and a sense of impermanency. The tri-county unit slowly eroded and was dismantled by 1982. As the report summed up, "Our goals were set during a time of easy money and radical change. The political and social climate has since changed." The impact of such climatic changes on women's practice styles is the focus of the following sections.

Overview of Individual Programs

Each of the four programs we interviewed began operations in the period of 1982 to 1985. These start-up dates tell us much about organizational experience and organizational politics. The women's movement was at a lower ebb then than in 1978. The lack of feminist networks in most rural Appalachian counties helped to shape the development and philosophy of these programs. Four interrelated factors help to account for what shape the programs took: boards, staffing, approaches to the community, and feminist connections. A strong relation exists between the rural context and the dimensions of organizational politics both within programs and within communities.

The dominant force in the establishment and maintenance of each of the battered-women's programs we examined has come from professional and community service providers. Each program began with small state grants and funding efforts. One program, for instance, conducted a raffle for an afghan and made $133.00. The director reports, "My mom won it; she was encouraged to buy so many tickets." Another program began with a $13,000.00 grant and hired a part-time director for $7,500 who worked full-time to get things going. Each of these programs began by offering telephone crisis services and provided shelter by working with local motels or renting a house. Today three of them own or rent a shelter facility while one continues to provide shelter at a local motel. Annual operating budgets range today from $60,000 to $114,000. Funding sources include federal, state, and local monies as well as foundations and fundraisers. Programs have conducted dances, fashion shows, golf tournaments, and phone-athons in search of additional funds. The funding climate is only one of the great difficulties activist women face in Appalachia. Only $450,000 was allocated for battered-women's services for the state as a whole in the locality studied. In contrast, Massachusetts allocated $8,300,000 to services for battered women the same year. This funding disparity constricts the political vision of rural programs as energy is directed to maintaining basic skeletal services. Paid staff ranges from two and 2/3 to four. All programs rely heavily on volunteers to provide services with most of the programs reporting a core of eight volunteers. Small budgets and small staffs, along with the rural environments of the programs, shape their political missions.

Politics from Within: Structure and Internal Dynamics

Board composition is often a key indicator of organizational politics. Each of the women's programs surveyed had men on their boards. Two of them had male board chairs. One program stated that it seeks a balance with no more than 50% males at a time. Only one program had an ex-battered woman represented on the board; the same program was also the only one with an active service volunteer on the board. In women's service organizations we have been familiar with outside the mountains, men have not been on boards since board membership is viewed as an important opportunity to promote women's leadership. Additionally, several of the programs emphasized the need for boards to possess "social polish." As one program director stated, "We need to be business-minded as an agency and look to people in the community who have power and influence and who can get to those people with money." Another said, "We needed the protection; especially at first, I got threatening phone calls at home." Since in these programs boards determine policy, board composition is an important influence on program politics.

The program staff we interviewed talked extensively about board activities. "It's like a Chinese fire drill. The board doesn't know what it needs until it happens." Boards often make policy under duress. "We are all starting out green. We can get better attendance from our women. Our board has done lots of soulsearching about hierarchy, power, control." Tensions erupt over director-board relations, board representation, and political strategy. Issues of personnel policy are often the most contested terrains. In each of the programs surveyed, an informal interpretation of board-written policy exists among staffers. All programs described board-staff relations as amicable but as one program director put it, "We haven't come to any real crunch yet."

The hiring of staff is a decision ultimately made by boards with varying degrees of input from staff. Board-staff disagreements over hiring have occurred in two of the programs. Three of the programs report that professional degrees for staffmembers are somewhat important but not the sole criterion. Most of the staff in each of the organizations have professional degrees. Out of twelve total staff members in the four programs, only five were from the communities served. One of the programs accounted for three of the five "locals." One of the programs serving a large population of Native Americans had no Native American staffmembers. As one staffer put it, "We have never had such a foreign crowd around here. Yet none of us were summer residents. We moved here and got right into the community and that's made all the difference." One program director noted that the "rapid Northern clip" of one staffer was an issue for the local community.

Problems from Outside: The Quicksand of Funding, Community Legitimacy, and Feminist Commitment

Each of the programs we studied share a similar philosophical approach to their local communities. This approach can be characterized as cautious and low key. "Our focus has been to be friendly but to chip away slowly." "It's a small town and we often see them socially." The extensive comments of one director reveal the particular difficulties and constraints women activists face in small, rural communities: "We play the game. We don't step on toes. We all have to live together, but there comes a point when you have to take a stance. Especially in a community like this, we work within the system. We are safe if we have a good relationship with the community. If we are a thorn in the side of the male population, we endanger our women. We are a business and very political. We walk the fence. If you bristle lots of people, then you can't bring up issues again for three or four years." Another reports that they "work hard to dispel the image that we are militant man-hating lesbians. There are people who would love to hang that label on us."

Despite their cautious approaches, these programs still rock the boat. Some of the tensions that have erupted include neighbors protesting the location of a shelter on their street. "These neighbors were the same people who originally donated blankets and sheets. Now they yell, 'We don't want white trash here.'" Other issues include ruffled feathers at the courthouse, cases involving abusers who have power and status in the community, and competition with mainstream agencies over turf. One program staffer described her conflict with agency directors as "arm wrestling with two male directors."

Each of the programs sees their rural contexts as posing special problems for their survival and work. Transportation, lack of phones, a lesser tax base for funding than in metropolitan areas, and the lack of political clout and voting constituency statewide given the low populations of the counties served were some of the problems mentioned. Additionally, underemployment and unemployment in the localities were discussed. One of the counties served had a medium income of only $6,000 in 1987. Strong desire on the part of many local women to stay put because of regional ties and allegiance to the land was also perceived as a special factor influencing service options. Program directors mentioned problems of isolation, especially during their start-up phase. One program consulted battered-women workers in an urban program for advice in setting up 24-hour crisis coverage. Reports the director: "They told me they were using an answering service. We don't have anything like that here." Other constraints mentioned were the trial courts and the problem of not being able to generate as many client statistics as urban programs for funding.

Speaking of their rural location, one program staffer said, "I see our location as a blessing and a hindrance." Lack of anonymity is one such mixed blessing. Each of the programs has carefully cultivated community credibility. Some have taken referrals for service not related to their mission in order to cement relationships within the community. Another has baked cookies for the police department as a peace offering to smooth out a problematic situation. All of the programs have invested much time and energy in strategizing to win community support and in responding to legitimation crises.

Without an extensive women's constituency and a strong feminist base of support, community approval is essential to program survival. The strong need to gain and maintain community support has tended to soften the feminist thrust of these programs and it has resulted in some distancing from the feminist movement. In response to questions regarding feelings toward the women's movement, many of the staff members were concerned about the "prolesbian" stances associated with feminism. They perceive that an emphasis on such issues would be polarizing in their communities. One program director states, "I'm not from any feminist theory background. Consensus theory doesn't work for me." In each of the programs, concern was expressed over "feminist tactics." As one worker said, "I'm not an activist. My approach is different than marching. To continue to make change within the system, we can't be pushy. We have to be tactful." Another states, "We have to be low-key here. I have to choose my issues; we are further behind in this community. We are the only thing for women. We are leaders yet we can't change the world here — just educate them that there is a different way. In sum, workers in these agencies tend to agree: "We don't take a radical feminist stance."

Summary

In a less than ideal environment given the lack of a funding base and an inability to gather support from alliances with other feminist groups due to their absence —battered-women's programs in rural Appalachia nonetheless produce a significant ideological challenge to male violence and help to shape institutional responses to battered women. With their entry in local organizations such as Rotary Clubs, these programs, as Schechter (1982:320) points out for programs elsewhere, have "raised a symbol for freeing women from brutality that has captured the attention of a far wider network than feminist." As with early women organizers in the South, the obstacles and contradictions movement women face must be considered. The fact that the strategies for change may differ from "Take Back the Night" marches in large cities to fashion shows in rural communities does not undermine the fact that both are effectively challenging the status quo of male privilege.

As Schechter (p. 320) points out, "the battered women movement has effectively used models built upon moral persuasion, consciousness-raising, and public education. The movement took the facts of women's daily lives, politically reinterpreted them, and insisted upon concrete changes." In the tradition of early organizing women, today's counterparts continue in their adaptations to the local climate.

Many of the problems that plague rural-based programs are no strangers to urban programs nor to the feminist movement. Amidst a backdrop of fiscal cutbacks and reactionary backlash, the role of men in the movement, leadership dilemmas, the importance of expediency, and the correct process and tactics for change are ongoing questions for women involved in social change activities. As Schechter (p. 291) has stated, "To take on the tasks ahead, the battered women movement needs to strengthen itself internally. The organization must develop visions of the future, clarify why they want to move in these directions, and devise concrete plans for getting there. Individual programs need to devote significant energy in solving organizational problems and clarifying structure and process." The politics of women's organizations do not remain static nor are they clear-cut. Their process of development is evolutionary. As with the early women organizers in Appalachia, the labels of "conservative" or "progressive" cannot be easily affixed.

REFERENCES

Kessler-Harris, Alice. *Women Have Always Worked.* NY: Feminist Press, 1981.

Schechter, Susan. *Women and Male Violence: The Visions and Struggles of the Battered Women's Movement.* Boston: South End Press, 1982.

Scott, Anne. *Making the Invisible Women Visible.* Urbana: University of Illinois Press, 1984.

Sullivan, Gail. "Cooptation of Alternative Services: The Battered Women's Movement as a Case Study." *Catalyst: A Socialist Journal of the Social Services.* Volume IV, 2 (1982): 39-58.

Tierney, Kathleen. "The Battered Women's Movement and the Creation of the Wife Beating Problem." *Social Problems.* Volume 29,3 (February) 1982: 207-20.

Whisnant, David. *All That Is Native and Fine.* Chapel Hill: University of North Carolina Press, 1983.

POETRY READING
Convenor: Roberta Herrin, East Tennessee State University
"The Women of Brasstown"
Bettie Sellers, Young Harris College
Yearning Toward Home and Its Traditions
Bennie Lee Sinclair, Cleveland, South Carolina
October Duck
Rita S. Quillen, East Tennessee State University
Selected Works From *Watauga Draw Down*
Don Johnson, East Tenneessee State University

Yearning Toward Home and Its Traditions

The idea of "home" is central to Appalachian culture, whether we refer to the region as "home," or the individual house as "home." Our churches have "homecomings," our families have reunions at the "homeplace." In South Carolina, the upstate Craig family has an annual gathering on the shore of Lake Keowee-Toxaway, on a point closest to the ancestral home now inundated by nuclear power plant lake waters. Today such "homesickness" takes many unique forms in our mountains. Families who sold their land to follow the job market find themselves unable to buy back into their native region, land prices having escalated to be affordable only to "outlanders." Much of the poetry that I write deals with the theme of yearning toward home and its traditions.

Decoration Day

This first Sunday in June, this green
first Sabbath of June, has long been designated
for the cleaning of graves. Each program
is the same: everyone brings rake, hoe, some
flowers, and, after preaching, climbs
this stubbled hill to find wiregrass
and weeds have taken ground since June's
first Sunday past; wild vines
and briars choke the rose and dahlia
left of last year's tending.

Each pilgrim as of age assumes his role:
the old kneed deeply in ancestral

dust, upending spiny threats upon
their own sure home, while those of lesser
urgency resolve themselves unmossing faded

elegiacs. It is the young who take
no part. Escaping one by one to ride
the afternoon, they do not hear the gentle chime
of hand-tool hitting rock; this knelling
for green bones as well as brittle.

The Mourning Man
(My Father-In-Law At Sixty-Three)

When he was a boy in north Georgia
an old horse faltered and lay, unmissed,
until fur drifted back to him
in tufts, out of dried carcass. Now, it is he
who breaks, clogging a city.

Even his wife is thinning, in her own way.
Sitting before the screen, she no longer eats,
or laughs at fresh spring bodies
leaping for him off vases;
out of the magazines.

And so he studies how we young
propose ourselves without shame,
and at night he examines his dream
that we scavenge what he has shed,
stringing it out on our clotheslines.

If he ran stripped and alone, girls
would collect like moths at the windows,
needing his light, but afraid.
Panting, he sprawls among the dark hedges.
He knows rats nest in what he cannot save.

In the mornings, when she turns, her wasted rib-cage
sings for him like the faery breast-bone.
He suspects she is a harp
no craftsman could ever create;
her hair the perfect weave for its strings.
Sewers vibrate as clever rodents fight

for each strand. The bus ceases to stop
in front of the store where he worked
now curling back from the sidewalk,
out of business.

Somewhere under the concrete
pungent fields he once knew
are unable to heave loose.
Whenever she moves, her music is deafening.
And he waits, each day an elegy.

"Why the Last Reunion Was"

To have his woodbin filled
after standing empty so long
made the old man whistle and hum;
and having his sons back home
at last he peeled his sweaters
and cleansed himself by their fire
proud as Abraham of his own
all sleeping now by the fire.
he tended before he would rest
stoking the chimney's shared song
out of joy as it whistled and roared
through other abandoned nests
of sweeps or wren
into frame as dry as his own

denied such warmth too long.

Threnody

At Bobby Garren's Cafe
not much has changed:
the dishes, chipped and crazed, rest
in a 1940's cabinet
above a rusted R.C. cooler,
the jukebox sings;

and I am seven again
on a barstool beside my daddy, waitresses hovering,
his black hair, blue eyes, pale skin

irresistable as stardust.
Close by, outside the dusky glass it waits,
a foreshortening

that will distort span, intent, and reasonsing—
but here, the runaway is safe.
Not much has changed.
The jukebox sings.

Fire Out of Hand

A middle-aged woman stokes
the backyard garbage can
of left-overs, bills due, trends,

and once she has seen them to ash
wanders back into the house
unaware of the power of flame
to consume out of what has been.
A scrap, a spark, some wind. . . fire
out of hand!

If only she'd look out the window
but with the children gone
her lawn seems incredibly vast, a reach

she'd rather not dream upon
as she climbs the stairs to her room
to nap what time till he's home,

her diminishing husband.
And up the neglected path
it comes, a crackle and snap, an aurora

so hungry for death
her heart from its sleep world warns her—
Yes! We struggle, we break, we change

but some things are ever the same, worth
our sorrow: this garden, these flowers, spring.
his love as needful as yours

in this stand against age and pain
if only you'd look
outside outside outside

yourself— an inferno
scaling the backporch steps, the trellis,
igniting the frenzied wasps' nests

their dying
unobserved as her own heart's breath
she has not listened to for years

asleep, adrift, alone;
and perhaps she will not now awake
until it has come down the hall,

blocked all exits. Fire
out of hand.

The Evangelist

Each summer, the alien evangelist comes
to do for us
what we cannot do for ourselves.
Sometimes, he is from Memphis;
sometimes, from Tucson;
but always his skill is superior.

Bennie Lee Sinclair, poet laureate of South Carolina, lives in the mountains near Cleveland with her husband, potter Don Lewis.

UNIVERSALITY IN LITERATURE
  Convenor: Parks Lanier, Radford University
Crimes Against Nature: The Image of The Mountaineer In Deliverance
  Rodger Cunningham, Sue Bennett College
R'lyeh In Appalachia: Lovecraft's Influence On Fred Chappell's Dagon
  Amy Tipton Gray, Caldwell Community College and Technical Institute
Teaching Jesse Stuart's "Dawn Of Remembered Spring"
  Danny L. Miller, Northern Kentucky University
Post Modern Appalachian Fiction
  Nancy C. Joyner, Western Carolina University

R'lyeh in Appalachia: Lovecraft's Influence on Fred Chappell's Dagon

by
Amy Tipton Gray

Throughout most of his career Fred Chappell has suffered the fate of the prophet who stays in and in his case, writes about his own land. While his early novels in particular have enjoyed success overseas, and have earned him such honors as the 1971 Prix de Meilleurs des Lettres Etrangeres (awarded for Dagon) recognition in his own country has been slow in coming (Ragan 37-38). In fact, only his most recent novel, *I Am One Of You Forever*, published over twenty years after his first, has received any sort of general critical acclaim. The same is not true of his poetry, which has attracted a wider and more appreciative audience and for which he has been the recipient of many awards, including the 1985 Bollinger Prize. It would be easy to assume, then, that Chappell's success as a poet names him a failure as a novelist. This is most emphatically not the case. For it is in Chappell's first three novels that themes of his poetry are first explored, and many of the problems in his early writing (prose as well as poetry) are worked out. Moreover, *Dagon* is clearly the pivotal work in Chappell's early corpus. It embodies both the culmination and resolution of Chappell's early difficulties, and points the way to the superior work that will follow. But in addition to suffering from Chappell's characteristic experiments with theme and style, *Dagon* has consistently been either dismissed or misinterpreted because of the writer's use of names and incantations taken from the Cthulhu mythos invented by H.P. Lovecraft. Such misapprehension must be cleared up before the novel can be appreciated for what it is: something more significant than just one more story about the reappearance of Lovecraft's mythical continent R'Lyeh, couched in this case in just one more of Chappell's difficult and unappealing first novels.

It is easy to discern the reasons for the unpopularity of Chappell's early work, especially *Dagon*. For Chappell "is an experimental novelist, a designation he himself has acknowledged" (Ragan 38). To use his own term, he is "a writer of the arabesque." Quillen quotes Chappell's definition of such a writer as one who "is less concerned with delivering basic narrative materials than with manipulating these materials in an idiosyncratic manner." A writer of the arabesque provides "a satisfactory narrative outline" and "then manipulates the elements so that the train of his narrative becomes of secondary importance" (Quillen 42-43). Most readers who are not interested in postmodernist theory and who buy books precisely because what they want is a good ride on that narrative train, find little in this technique to recommend. And when combined with unsympathetic and unappealing characters, abstruse symbolism and obscure allegory, and an unrelenting exposition of the dark side of human nature, the novel of the arabesque is practically a surefire failure. Which critically, of course, Chappell's first three novels were.

Dagon was called by one critic "another horse from the dilapidated stable of the Southern Gothic novel" (Buitenhuis). Another wrote, "There is nothing here to commend it to libraries" (Cohen). It was accused of being both a gothic retread and an unprofitable reworking of the Lovecraftian vein. A summary of the plot quickly demonstrates why Dagon has suffered these epithets. The novel opens with a quotation that proves indecipherable to anyone who is not familiar with the work of Lovecraft: "Ph'nglui mglw'nafh Cthulhu R'lyeh wgah'nagl fhtagn " A prolonged search will eventually lead to "The Call of Cthulhu," which yields this unhelpful translation: "In his house at R'lyeh dead Cthulhu waits dreaming" (140). After passing that arcane beginning, the reader pushes on to learn that, true to Chappell's then favorite form, the basic plot of the novel is simple to outline-- once it has been unearthed.

Peter Leland, a minister, inherits an old house and decides to take a leave of absence from his ministry to write a book titled *Remnant Pagan Forces In American Puritanism*, a topic inspired by William Bradford's account of the Merry Mount (Mount Dagon) incident. Once he and his wife Sheila have moved in, Peter discovers a horde of old documents stored in the house, documents that are filled with words such as "Shoggoth." "Pnakotic," "Nyarlath," and "Nephreu" (which, as the only word not found in Lovecraft's stories, may well be Chappell's own contribution to the pantheon). He also discovers his neighbor Mina Morgan, with whom he immediately becomes erotically obsessed. As Peter falls more and more under the spell of both Mina and the old papers, he begins to personify one of the major themes of Chappell's early work, the struggle between will and appetite. Eventually, appetite is victorious. Peter, angered by Sheila's insistence that he kill a snake (what else?), kills his wife instead and moves in with Mina, who ensures the triumph of appetite by drugging him with sex and moonshine until he becomes devoid of will, both literally and figuratively impotent.

At this point the Lovecraftian elements of the story take on a new twist Mina finds a new man to serve as an acolyte of sorts; they pour Peter into his car and take him to the seaport town of Gordon (perhaps Chappell's pun on the famous frozen fish company). There she hires two whores, and the four of them proceed to tattoo Peter's entire body while simultaneously reducing him to a child-like state. When the tattooing is finished, Mina has Peter taken to an altar where he is sacrificed before a maimed and truncated fertility deity Dagon. But Peter maintains his identity throughout the encounter, welcomes his sacrificial death instead of fighting it, and after dying gains a profound and detached understanding of the universe. He is transformed into Leviathan. the cosmic fish (perhaps the only aquatic being to escape Lovecraft), and settles into eternity: "joyfully bellowing, he wallowed and sported upon the rich darkness that flows between the stars" *(Dagon* 177).[1]

In the face of such evidence. it is easy to see why many have believed that *Dagon* should as a matter of course be subsumed into the Lovecraftian genre, especially since Lovecraft himself "encouraged other writers to write stories in his framework" (DeCamp 331). However, although Chappell and Lovecraft employed the same set of entities, both the purpose to which each put these creatures and the effect each was trying to achieve were widely disparate. Furthermore, while it can be said that critics such as S.T. Joshi (whose area of expertise is Lovecraft criticism) are correct in stating that "Chappell's *Dagon*... [strives] not to imitate slavishly Lovecraft's own plots," it cannot be asserted, as Joshi goes on to do, that Chappell sought "to elaborate on [Lovecraft's] ideas" (Joshi 25).

Lovecraft, an admirer of Poe and the eighteenth century, sought to revitalize horror fiction and bring it out of the disreputable corner of American letters in which it had so long sat. While he did not accomplish this goal, he did succeed in both redefining the genre and influencing the generation of writers who succeeded him (which included Robert E Howard and Stephen King). Lovecraft's genius was two-fold. First, he "firmly attached the emotion of spectral dread to such concepts as outer space...and alien beings," transferring "the focus of supernatural" anxiety "from man and his little world and his gods, to the stars and the black and unplumbed gulfs of...space" (Lieber 290-292). Second, he created a pantheon of monsters who, unlike any found in any horror story written up to that time, were absolutely indifferent to mankind. These powerful fish-beings had fallen to earth from somewhere in space to rule the planet from R'lyeh, the continent that sank beneath the sea upon their eventual overthrow. All but oblivious to the existence of that piti-

---

[1]This is as good a point as any to note that despite its lack of success when it was first released in 1968, *Dagon* has recently been reissued and now graces the shelves of grocery stores and K-Marts. One can only speculate what its reappearance has to say about the changes the past two decades have wrought in American popular culture.

ful animal man, they were concerned only with using the priests and priestesses of their ancient cult to regain their former kingdom.

The invention of these viscoid creatures marks a major development in the world of science fiction. Before Lovecraft, even monsters from outer space had deliberate, personal reasons for wreaking havoc on the earth. Lovecraft, however, understood that true horror lies in the meaningless, pointless attack, in the fear peculiar to the twentieth century: the fear of being destroyed by something that cannot even be said to be uncaring, something that does not know or even think it is important to know who its victim is.

But the monsters of the mythos served another purpose in Lovecraft's fiction. Lovecraft believed that "the cosmos" was neither "basically inimicable" nor "beneficial to man" (Mosig 105). To this end he employed his creatures as metaphors for a dispassionate universe. Lovecraft, "a mechanistic materialist," saw man as merely another tiny accident in a universe full of tiny accidents, perpetually the victim of forces he neither understands nor controls. From this belief comes "the source of terror in Lovecraft's tales" (Joshi 20). The grotesque beings of the mythos highlight what their creator perceives to be man's insignificance in a "universe revealed by materialistic science" to be a "purposeless soulless place" (Leiber 293). That most men would go mad if they were forced to face the true nature of reality is a matter of no great concern to Lovecraft. One should simply accept the fact that philosophy is an illusion, that human action is unimportant, and carry on.

Most critics, either knowing little or nothing of Lovecraft's philosophy or being unwilling to accept it, have focused on the creatures themselves rather than on the function they were designed to serve. Some critics have even gone so far as to impose their own religious beliefs, specifically traditional Christian doctrine, on a fictional system that patently did not support such interpretation. There is no redemption, not even existential, in the ethos upon which Lovecraft based his work.

Furthermore, Lovecraft's style, which even his devotees sometimes have difficulty admiring, has also contributed to the misinterpretation of his work. His admiration for Poe and the eighteenth century (which has been well documented) gave him his literary voice, a voice that does not speak in accents pleasing to the twentieth century ear. Unlike Chappell, he was no experimenter; he found nothing in the new to be recommended. Instead he strove to reproduce in his works a "style... in vogue in the Romantic era much used by Poe and his Gothic predecessors" (Faig). In this he succeeded; so much so that in many ways his work provides an almost faultless reproduction of the gothic style. His writing is verbose, difficult, inflated, and full of lurid, polychrome adjectives. His stories are set in mysterious old houses (the American version of the crumbling castle) by the sea; his plots overflow with violence and terror. His characters are flat. All motivation is exterior. And the plot invariably builds to a "terminal climax" by means of "confirmation rather than revelation" (Lieber 297).

Chappell, on the other hand, consistently has been praised for the clarity of his prose and the beauty of his descriptions. The motivation of his characters is interior; it is the war man fights against himself that fascinates Chappell. While he too has a fondness for old houses, his settings usually serve an allegorical purpose, unlike the mansions of Lovecraft, which function only as dilapidated props. Moreover, it is ironic that the difficulties in Chappell's works have come about because of his enthusiasm for experiment, while Lovecraft's stories suffer from that author's attempts to recreate the style of an age long past.

Thus it is neither archaic diction, nor a slavish adherence to the gothic, that has caused *Dagon's* troubles. For in addition to suffering from the troubles that typically hound experimental novels, the book has consistently resisted classification. Despite its setting, it certainly could not be called an Appalachian novel, for its characters not to mention its plot do not fall into the patterns outlined by Cratis Williams, Isabel D. Harris and others. In addition, Chappell, by choosing a fictional mythos upon which to pin his narrative, effectively cut off his novel from a group of its contemporaries to which it could have easily belonged. Gardner's *Grendel*, Updike's *Centaur*, Barth's *Chimera* and even Mailer's *Ancient Evenings*, to name a few, all are based on reinterpretation of traditional mythologies. The key word, of course, is traditional; because of Cthulhu and company, *Dagon* was labeled, understandably science fiction. And with equal immediacy, it was dismissed as not being worthy of serious study.

The original idea for *Dagon* came not from Lovecraft, however, but from William Bradford. As Chappell puts it, "I discovered a literal event in Bradford's *History of the Plymouth Colony* which seemed to me to be metaphorically true of our own times. To drag Bradford's reported event into the present I posited a secret religious cult which had survived unseen for two centuries" (Chappell "Six Propositions"). And the cult of Cthulhu, of which Dagon is a deity, is the cult that for better or worse came to Chappell's mind.

But Chappell used Lovecraft's mythos not because he sought to write a horror story, but because he saw it as a powerful metaphor for man's interior struggle against evil (will against appetite), a struggle that must be manifested in the material world. Balanced between Calvin and Camus, Chappell believes that each individual is responsible for making sense of original sin (defined as a set of conditions existing before the characters come on the scene) in his own terms. Darkness triumphs only when man refuses to recognize the limitations with which he has no choice but to live, and refuses to work within those limitations. Unlike Lovecraft, Chappell does not believe philosophy is a comforting illusion maintained in the teeth of a meaningless existence. For this reason, Chappell went against all advice and refused to remove the final scene, in which Peter becomes Leviathan, from the novel. He could not, he said, "accept the triumph of evil that way in the world," and could not end *Dagon* without an attempt "to alleviate the agony of it" (Ragan 45).

The final evidence that Chappell is neither thrashing out another southern gothic nor reworking Lovecraft lies in the definition of the romance as set out by Richard Chase in *The American Novel and Its Tradition*. Chase states that the characters in a romance "will on the whole be shown in ideal relation. . . they will share emotions only after they have become abstract or symbolic." When such characters do "become profoundly involved in some way," as Peter Leland does with Mina, they can only experience "a deep, narrow, and obsessive involvement." All moves towards abstraction and idealism. And as it is "less committed to the immediate rendition of reality" than other types of works, "the romance will more freely veer toward mythic allegorical and symbolistic forms" (Chase 13). What better description can be found of Dagon, or indeed, of Chappell's early work as a whole?

It is clear that Chappell's *Dagon* should not be catalogued with the works of L. P. Lovecraft. While Chappell employs the names and incantations invented by Lovecraft in the rituals performed for the god Dagon, he does so with a purpose that goes far beyond Lovecraft's original intent. Chappell, unconcerned with intensifying the horror factor, imbues these figures with a symbolic power not found in the original stories for which they were created. In doing so Chappell dislodges his readers from their comfortable assumptions about reality and forces them to face what is darkest in themselves. From Lovecraft's perspective, man was merely a minuscule victim of forces beyond his cognizance; self-knowledge was of no help in deflecting the violence perpetuated by an amoral cosmos. To this end he used the characters from the Cthulhu mythos to give a new form to the horror story, for in his work, the terror comes from outside man's experience from external, indifferent beings rather than from within man's own being.

This is not true of Chappell, who believes that man, torn between will and appetite, can only resolve that struggle through self-knowledge; this is also the only means by which he can come to a resolution about the nature of the world and his place in it. In Chappell's cosmos conflict arises from each person's inner struggle to balance the opposing forces that beset us all. In Lovecraft's world, these forces are unimportant; one man's inner conflict means nothing when placed beside the devastation that can be on humanity by ancient forces, manifested in weird creatures beyond its ken. In short, Lovecraft's lexicon does not include the concept of hope; there is no escape from Cthulhu.

But Chappell, through Peter and Leviathan, has shown us the way out of R'lyeh.

WORKS CITED

Chappell, Fred. *Dagon*. New York: Harcourt, Brace and World, 1968.

"Six Propositions About Literature and History." *New*Literary History, 1 (Spring 1970): 513-522.

de Camp, L. Sprague. *Lovecraft: A Biography*. Garden City, New York:Doubleday, 1975.

Faig, Kenneth W. Jr., and S.T. Joshi. "H.P. Lovecraft: His Life andWork." In *H.P. Lovecraft: Four Decades of Literary Criticism*. Ed. S.T. Joshi. Athens, Ohio: Ohio University Press, 1980.

Lieber, Fritz, Jr. "A Literary Copernicus." *The Acolyte*, Fall 1944. Rpt. and revised in *Something About Cats and Other Pieces* by H.P. Lovecraft. Ed. August Derleth. Freeport, New York: Books for Libraries Press, 1949; reprinted 1971 by arrangement with Scott Meredith Literary Agency, Inc.: 290-303.

Lovecraft, H.P. "The Call of Cthulhu." *Weird Tales*, Feb. 1928. Rpt. in *The Dunwich Horror and Others: The Best Supernatural Stories of H.P. Lovecraft*. Ed. August Derleth. Sauk City, Wisconsin: Arkham House, 1963: 130-159.

Mosig, Dirk W. "H.P. Lovecraft: Myth-Maker." In *I Miti di Cthulhu* .Eds. August Derleth et al. [Italy]: n.p.:n.p., 1976. Rpt. in *Whispers*, Dec. 1976; copyright Stuart David Schiff. Revised and rpt. in *The Miskatonic*, Feb. 1976, copyright Dirk W. Mosig. Rpt. in *H.P. Lovecraft: Four Decades of Literary Criticism*. Ed. S.T. Joshi. Athens, Ohio: Ohio University Press, 1980: 186-190.

Quillen, Rita S. "Looking For Native Ground: The Appalachian Poetry of Fred Chappell and Jim Wayne Miller." *Appalachian Heritage*, No. 2 (Spring 1980): 42-55.

Ragan, David Paul. "Chappell, Fred." *Dictionary of Literary Biography*.Vol. 6 of *American Novelists Since World War II Second Series*. Ed. James E. Kibler, Jr. Detroit: Gale Research Company Book Tower, 1980: 36-48.

ECONOMIC DEVELOPMENT AND REDEVELOPMENT
Convenor: Tom Shannon, Radford University
The Rayon Mills in Elizabethton, Tennessee: A Case Study of Appalachian Economic Development, 1926-1970
  Marie Tedesco, East Tennessee State University
  Norma Thomas, East Tennessee State University
Regional Redevelopment Strategies: The Comparative Case of Catalonia, Spain
  Glenn Mitchell, Warren Wilson College
Deck The Hills: Christmas Tree Farms and Economic Development in the High Country of Avery County, North Carolina
  Elizabeth C. Stevens, Appalachian State University
Transylvania Goodpasture and The Industrialization of Smyth County, Virginia
  Glenna Horne Graves, Appalachian Center, University of Kentucky

The Rayon Plants In Elizabethton, Tennessee: A Case Study of Appalachian Economic Development, 1920-1985

by
Marie Tedesco

In August 1925 local newspapers carried the announcement that J.P. Bemberg Company, Barmen, Germany was to construct a plant in Elizabethton, Tennessee for the manufacture of "artificial silk," or rayon as it came to be called. Bemberg, an affiliate of Vereinigte Glanzstoff Fabriken (VGF), Elberfeld, Germany, was one of the world's leading manufacturers of rayon. Because the recently enacted (1922) Fordney-McCumber Tariff had included rayon as one of the protected "infant industries," imported rayon was too expensive for the average consumer. The German firm thus sought to avoid this high tariff by making rayon in the United States. Groundbreaking for the plant occurred in September 1925, and approximately 13 months later, in October 1926, the American Bemberg factory began production of rayon by the cuprammonium process. Two years later a companion plant, American Glanzstoff, also operated by VGF, began production of rayon by the viscose process.[1]

Establishment of the rayon factories in Elizabethton raises a number of questions. Why did one of the world's leading manufacturers of rayon choose Elizabethton, a small town of 2746 located in rural Carter County in East

Tennessee, for the site of two of its factories? How did civic and business leaders react to the Germans' plans? Over the years, how have the plants affected the economy of Elizabethton and Carter County? What does the experience of the plants in Elizabethton reveal about Appalachian economic development? It is the intent of this paper to analyze these questions, paying special attention to the economic impact of the plants on Elizabethton and Carter County. A number of factors convinced VGF to locate two of its plants in Elizabethton. The availability and purity of the water supply, availability of copper reserves (for the cuprammonium process) in southwest Virginia and east Tennessee, the promise of cheap labor, and community economic concessions convinced the German corporation to locate its cuprammonium plant in Elizabethton. The same factors, together with the prospect of obtaining a cheap source of cellulose through purchase of cotton linters from Georgia and North Carolina textile mills, convinced VGF to locate the viscose-process Glanzstoff factory in Elizabethton.[2]

Elizabethton's civic leaders were only too glad to have the factories locate in their town. Like civic leaders in other declining rural areas of the South, those in Elizabethton were infected with the spirit and ethos of the "New Era."[3] This 1920s emotional boosterism led Elizabethton's civic leaders—as well as those from nearby Johnson City—to court the German industrialists. Visions of a burgeoning, prosperous, metropolitan Elizabethton of 150,000 people encouraged these leaders to make numerous concessions to VGF, first for the Bemberg plant, and then for the Glanzstoff factory. These concessions are too numerous to detail in their entirety, but explication of the major ones will be sufficient to demonstrate that in essence civic leaders agreed to allow the plants to exploit the area's resources and its workers.

One of VGF's primary concerns was exemption from city and county property tax. Carter County granted both Bemberg and Glanzstoff ten-year exemption from paying county property tax. City officials, for their part, in 1925 agreed not to extend the corporate limits so as to include Bemberg. But in the event such extension did occur then Bemberg would be exempt from taxation for ten years. Two years later the Elizabethton and Johnson City chambers of commerce (hereafter referred to as the chambers) agreed to try to convince the state legislature to remove the Glanzstoff plant from within Elizabethton city limits. Apparently, the chambers succeeded because it was not until 1943 that the plant properties themselves were taxed. Prior to that time, the plants paid city tax on other properties they owned which lay within Elizabethton corporate limits.[4]

Other major concessions revolved around water—200 gallons of which were needed to manufacture one pound of rayon. The chambers agreed to pay the lesser of $10,000 or one-half the cost of erecting a filtration plant for Bemberg's use. Further, the chambers agreed to construct a water main from the Mountain Spring Water Company to the plant, and to guarantee that Bemberg would pay only $300 per year for water for the succeeding 25 years after the plant began operation. In addition, the chambers secured permission for Bemberg to use the waters of the Watauga River. Subsequently, the chambers consented to construct two new reservoirs in Elizabethton for city water service, and to allow Glanzstoff to use all water not needed by the city.[5]

Allowing the exploitation of natural resources, however, apparently was not the only concession the chambers made to the plants. In his 1949 study of Elizabethton, John Fred Holly contended that civic leaders presented corporate representatives a document which stated that they would never have to pay workers more than $10 per week. Other sources concede that the promise of an abundant, cheap supply of labor attracted the German industrialists, but no other source mentions this document shown to Holly by E.C. Alexander, city manager in 1925, and a member of both the Elizabethton Chamber of Commerce and the committee which negotiated to bring the plants to Elizabethton.[6]

At any rate, it seems clear that civic leaders willingly, indeed anxiously, participated in the exploitation of the region's human and natural resources. The wooing of Bemberg and Glanzstoff fits a model of neocolonial exploitation of Appalachia. In this case the civic leaders of Elizabethton and Johnson City themselves participated in, and arranged for, exploitation by a foreign corporation.[7]

No doubt local leaders willingly participated in this exploitation because Elizabethton and Carter County were in an area plagued by labor surpluses. Easily accessible timber resources, for example, had been depleted, causing local manufacturing concerns which had depended on timber to go out of business. Agriculture in the county always had been tenuous at best. There thus existed a sizeable supply of unskilled and semiskilled labor which could be employed in the factories.[8]

For Elizabethton and Carter County the rayon plants fulfilled the role of a "pioneer industry." In his study of postWorld War II industrial development in the southeast, Merrill L. Johnson defined a pioneer industry as one which first exposes a labor force to the industrial work place. Although there were some industrial firms in Elizabethton and Carter County prior to the establishment of the rayon plants, industrial employment was insignificant. Carter County in 1919 had 889 wage earners. By 1924 that number had declined to 742. The rayon factories became the first large scale industrial employer in the county and city.[9]

In accordance with Johnson's model, the rayon factories did bridge the gap between agricultural and industrial culture in Elizabethton and Carter County, the factories provided employment in a region which possessed an excess supply of lowskilled labor. But there was a major difference between the Johnson model and the Elizabethton situation. Typically, industries which demand little skill—cotton textiles, for example—fulfill the role of pioneers. Rayon manufacture, however, demands considerable skill. As Jack Blicksilver explained in his article on man-made fibers, the chemical preparation of viscose rayon demands scrupulous control of time, temperature and humidity. Moreover, the reaction between chemicals—ripened alkali cellulose and carbon bisulfide—must proceed at the proper pace else the resultant product will be useless.[10] It is testimony to the skills of Elizabethton and Carter County workers that they quickly learned the techniques necessary for rayon manufacture.

On October 28, 1926 the American Bemberg factory began producing cuprammonium rayon at the rate of 7,000 pounds per day. When, two years later, in September, 1928, American Glanzstoff began making viscose rayon, employment at the two plants topped 3,000. By the end of 1928, Bemberg, after losing $131,224 the previous year, turned a profit of $619,153.[11] Industrialists, civic leaders and workers alike thus were confident that both plants would be a successful part of the community for years to come.

But even before the stock market crash and the ensuing Great Depression caused widespread despair about the state of the American economy and the future of the rayon plants, two strikes which lasted from March through May 1929, engendered much bitterness and resentment on the part of the workers toward Bemberg and Glanzstoff. It is not the intent of this paper, however, to analyze the strike, especially since it has been well-documented, most recently by Jacquelyn D. Hall in the September 1986 issue of the *Journal of American History*. Suffice it to say that the struggle over low pay and long hours waged by the then predominantly female labor force, for many left a legacy of bitterness and distrust. The civic and business leaders of Elizabethton, along with the governor of Tennessee, cooperated with the industrialists, led by the plants' president, Arthur Mothwurf, to put down the strike and to deny the workers redress of their grievances.[12]

The strike of course cost the plants lost production, and the workers lost wages. But before the workers or the plants could fully recover from the effects of the strike, the American economy went into a tailspin, beginning in October of 1929. During the ensuing depression, the plants stayed afloat, 'though there were cutbacks in wages and employment. For the years 1931-39 the mean number of workers employed at the factories was 3294, with the lowest number of 2491 employed in 1932, and the highest of 4588 employed in 1939. Total payrolls bottomed out in 1932 ($2,761,595), while average annual wages and salaries bottomed out in 1934 at $1,000. During this same period net sales and pounds of rayon produced fluctuated until 1939, when they began a steady ascent through the war years.[13]

Reduced production at the plants, and reduced payrolls, naturally had an adverse effect on Elizabethton and Carter County. Retail sales in the county, for example, declined steadily from 1929 through 1933. Plant payrolls, meanwhile, began to turn upward in 1932.[14] During this same period of time, available statistics for American Bemberg show that after earning a net profit of $619,153 in 1928, Bemberg lost $499,832 in 1929, $482,498 in 1931, $603,619 in 1933, and $493,650 in 1934. In 1936 Bemberg again realized a net profit, this time of $598,161. From then through the end of the depression in 1939, Bemberg made a profit. It is interesting to note, however, that from 1933 through 1941 Bemberg and Glanzstoff (as of 1934 North American Rayon) stocks reported dividends.[15]

Locally, one major casualty of the depression was the demise of Watauga Development Corporation (WDC), a realty company which had been organized in 1925 by Elizabethton business leaders and Bemberg interests for the purpose of selling houses and/or land to plant employees. WDC overextended itself in the period immediately following the announcement of Bemberg's locating in Elizabethton. To finance land purchased at boom prices of $500 and more per acre, WDC borrowed money, and bought real estate on time at 6% interest. But WDC never was able to sell as much land or as many houses as it had hoped to because many plant employees chose either to commute from their rural homes, or to build in rural areas near their kin. By the time the depression hit, WDC's assets were tied up in unimproved farm land, and it was forced into bankruptcy. The lands were taken over by the mortgage holder, while the houses were taken over by the plants under a second mortgage.[16]

The demands of World War II necessitated increased production, and hence payrolls and employment also increased. Until that happened, assessment of the plants' economic impact on Elizabethton and Carter County is mixed-even when taking into account the Great Depression. As a foreign corporation profits went overseas to Algemeene Kunstzijde Unie N.V. (AKU), the Dutch company formed by VGF and another Dutch firm, N.V. Nederlandsche Kunstzijde Fabriek in 1929. There's not much evidence that the plants were concerned with putting money back into the community.[17] But in the early 1930s Bemberg and Glanzstoff/North American did spend a great deal of money fighting suits which challenged the ten-year county and perpetual city tax exemptions earlier granted the factories. Carter County and Elizabethton lost considerable tax revenues because of these exemptions. Lost revenues (estimated by Holly to be at least $2,600,000) contributed to the city government being near bankruptcy in 1943. In that year the state legislature passed a law which allowed Elizabethton to collect taxes from Bemberg and North American.[18]

It is true, of course, that the plants were directly responsible for Elizabethton's population jumping from 2,746 in 1920 to 8,044 in 1930 and 8,516 in 1940. Moreover, the rayon factories provided thousands of jobs—even during the depths of the Great Depression. From 1931 through 1947, plant payrolls approached $115,000,000. Significantly Pearson's correlations between plant payrolls and retail sales in Carter County point to the strength of the relationship between the prosperity of the plants and that of the community as a whole.[19]

After the war, however, there were significant changes for Bemberg and North American. As early as 1942 the Office of Alien Property (OAP) had initiated an investigation of AKU's ownership of American Bemberg, North American Rayon and American Enko, looking toward a vesting of enemy owned (German) interests in these companies. Cooperation of the Dutch government in exile was sought, primarily because of the importance of AKU to the Dutch economy. OAP was ready to vest in 1944, but on the advice of the State Department delayed action, in anticipation of a future settlement with the Dutch. Finally, on August 7, 1947, AKU and the OAP came to an agreement which provided that the Dutch corporation waive all claim to shares of outstanding stock which it or its affiliates owned in Bemberg and North American, together with working capital, assets, and all of AKU's interests in patents, trademarks and other industrial property of the two companies. The companies remained under government control until their purchase by Beaunit Mills, Inc., a New York corporation, in December, 1948.[20]

At the time Beaunit bought the plants, Bemberg concentrated production on "Bemberg" rayon yarn, from which triple sheer rayon cloth used in women's clothing was made. North American produced viscose yarn, most of which was sold to the rayon woven goods industry, with some being sold to tire companies. Financially, both companies were in good condition, and both dominated the economy of Elizabethton and Carter County. As of 1949 the plants were still by far Elizabethton's and Carter County's largest employers. Bemberg employed 2100 workers, while North American employed 3900.[21]

Beginning in 1949, though, the plants entered into a long period of decline. In part this decline can be attributed to an overall decline in the growth in the South of such traditional low-wage industries as textiles (if rayon production is categorized with textiles).[22] But decline can be attributed more to trends in the synthetic fiber market. Although manmade fibers in general continued to make substantial gains during the 1950s, there were changes in what types of fibers made the gains. Cellulosics—including rayon—lost their hegemony of the man-made fiber industry, while the non-cellulosics gained. During the 1958 recession production of cellulosics was sharply curtailed, resulting in lost revenues for even the largest manufacturers. The chief beneficiary of these changes was nylon; the major loser, rayon.[23] Thus, the Elizabethton plants, producers of rayon only, faced a new economic reality in which the market for their product was shrinking. Beaunit thus switched part of the Bemberg plant to the manufacture of polyester, and part of the North American plant to nylon.[24]

Although in many instances interfiber competition was among divisions of the same company (as was true with DuPont and American Viscose, for example), the desire to get the competitive edge for the future and not be stuck with money-losing products frequently led companies into ill-fated ventures. This is what happened to Beaunit. In the early 1960s the company entered into an agreement with El Paso Natural Gas Company to finance a "nylon 6" plant at Etowah, Tennessee. Blicksilver observed that for Beaunit the venture was "in the nature of hedging their bet, should they guess wrong in their major emphasis on rayon."[25] As it turned out, the joint venture was a disaster for Beaunit. Prior to October 1, 1966 when the nylon plant became operational, Beaunit deferred joint venture costs as preproduction expenses. Once the plant became operational, this could not be done, and as a result Beaunit incurred significant losses.[26]

Other factors contributed to Beaunit's—and hence Bemberg's and North American's—woes. Increased domestic production of polyester, brought on by previous high profits, increased foreign competition, and reduction of the amount of polyester used in synthetic blends, reduced the price of polyester from 84 cents per pound in July 1966 to 58 cents per pound in May 1967. A 1967 strike by three major tire companies which decreased demand for tire rayon further hurt the Elizabethton factories.[27] With all its troubles, Beaunit shareholders in 1967 approved a merger which resulted in the company's becoming a wholly owned subsidiary of El Paso Natural Gas Company. By that time employment at the plants had declined to 3500—down substantially from the 6000 of 1949.[28]

As the plants declined, though, other industries moved into Elizabethton, and the economy of the area diversified. In 1947 only 308 persons were employed in industries other than rayon manufacture, but in 1969 that number had increased to 1032, and by 1973 to 1640.[29] In some respects, then, the decline of the plants helped produce a healthier, more diversified economy for Elizabethton and Carter County. No longer was the region so dependent on a single employer.

Bemberg, however, could not survive. In the early 1970s it was sold to an investment group, and for a few years thereafter operated as Bemberg Industries, Inc. In 1976 Bemberg filed for bankruptcy. North American made it through the troubled 1970s, first as a division of Beaunit, then, after 1976, as the property of TA Associates, the investment group which bought Beaunit from El Paso Company. By 1985, however, the outlook was bleak for North American. To save the company, employees voted in favor of an Employee Stock Option Plan (ESOP), and in December 1985 North American became an employee-owned company.[30]

The evolution of the company has thus been curious. From a factory owned by a foreign company concerned with circumventing high American tariffs, and maximizing profits by employing "cheap, native labor," North American has become an ESOP plant determined to save itself in an era when many American factories are finding it difficult to survive. The situation in Elizabethton, then, has turned out quite differently from that in many other Appalachian communities where companies have exploited the natural resources and the workers, and then abandoned the community. At least in part, North American and Elizabethton have escaped that fate.

ENDNOTES

1. John Fred Holly, "Elizabethton, Tennessee: A Case Study of Southern Industrialization," diss., Clark University, 1949, pp. 121-22; James A. Hodges, "Challenge to the New South: The Great Textile Strike in Elizabethton, Tennessee, 1929," *Tennessee Historical Quarterly*, 23(1964), 343-44; Frank Merritt, *Later History of Carter County, 1865-1980* (Homecoming '86 Heritage Project, 1986), p. 241; and Herman Robinson, "Monday 25th Anniversary of Bemberg," *Elizabethton Star* (ES), October 28, 1951, p. 3-8.

   The cuprammonium process uses a copper/ammonium solution for dissolving cellulose, while the viscose process uses lye and a compound of carbon and sulfur to convert the cellulose into a soluble compound. See Robert E. Hussey and Philip C. Scherer, "The Rayon Industry in the South," in *Chemical Progress in the South*, ed., J.E. Mills (New York: The Chemical Foundation, 1930), p. 136. On the development of the viscose process also consult Jack Blicksilver, "Man-Made Fibers. A Growth Industry for the Diversifying South," *Textile History Review*, 3(January 1962), 5-7.

   On the Fordney-McCumber Tariff see: George H. Soule, *Prosperity Decade. From War to Depression: 1917-1929* (New York: Holt, Rinehart, 1947), p. 131; and Frank W. Taussig, *Some Aspects of the Tariff Question. An Examination of the Development of American Industries Under Protection* (New York: AMS Press, 1971), pp. 426-27.

2. Holly, "Elizabethton," pp. 126-28; and Frank Bohn, "Tennessee's New Silkworm—Industrial Germany Comes to America," *Review of Reviews*, 78(October 1928), p. 368. The viscose process produced more rayon, and thus used more cellulose. There was a need, then, for a cheap source of cellulose, other than wood pulp.

3. On "New Era" boosterism of the 1920s in the South, see James C. Cobb, *Industrialism and Southern Society, 1877-1984* (Lexington, KY: University Press of Kentucky, 1984), pp. 32-34; and Blaine A. Brownell, *The Urban Ethos in the South, 1920-1930* (Baton Rouge, LA: Lousiana State University Press, 1975). A comparable movement took place in the 1950s and 1960s, this time involving more organized state directed efforts to attract industry to the South. See Cobb, *The Selling of the South: The Southern Crusade for Industrial Development, 1936-1980* (Baton Rouge, LA: Lousiana State University Press, 1982).

4. Holly, "Elizabethton," pp. 124-25, 129, 131-32. For the plants' payment of taxes on properties owned see "Rayon Plants Pay City Tax," *ES*, June 8, 1939,.p. 1.

5. Holly, "Elizabethton," pp. 126-27, 133.

6. Ibid, p. 134. Among the other sources which discuss the importance of the plants having a readily available supply of cheap labor are: Hodges, "Challenge to the New South," 345-46; Bohn, "Tennessee's New Silkworm," p. 368; A.J. Buttrey, "Salvation in Tennessee: The Clergy and the Textile Strikers," *The World Tomorrow*, 12 (October 1924), p. 396; Tom Tippett, *When Southern Labor Stirs* (New York: Jonathan Cape and Harrison Smith, 1930), pp. 56-57; and Jacquelyn D. Hall, "Disorderly Women: Gender and Labor Militancy in the Appalachian South," *Journal of American History*, 73 (September 1986), 359.

7. On the colonialism theory as it applies to Appalachia consult Helen M. Lewis and Edward E. Knipe, "The Colonialism Model: The Appalachian Case," in *Colonialism in Modern America: The Appalachian Case*, eds., Helen M. Lewis and Donald Askins (Boone, NC: The Appalachian Consortium Press, 1978); Richard B. Drake, "Jack and Clio in Appalachia: Comments on Regional Historiography," *Appalachian Notes*, First Quarter (1976), 1-8; and Ronald Eller, *Miners, Millhands, and Mountaineers. Industrialization of the Appalachian South, 1880-1930* (Knoxville,TN: University of Tennessee Press, 1982), xxv-xxvi.

In regard to foreign ownership, the Elizabethton plants-and American rayon plants in general—differed from textile plants in the South. As late as the 1920s, for example, 80-90% of Southern spindles were Southern owned. By contrast, the American rayon industry was dominated by foreign ownership because the technology for rayon manufacture was European and British in origin. On Southern textile ownership see Gavin Wright, *Old South. New South. Revolutions in the Southern Economy Since the Civil War* (New York: Basic Books, 1986), p.131. On rayon consult Blicksilver, "Man-Made Fibers," 20.

9. Johnson, "Postwar Industrial Development in the Southeast and the Pioneer Role of Labor-Itensive Industry," *Economic Geography*, 61(January 1985), 50; Holly, "Elizabethton," pp. 118-19.

10. Johnson, "Postwar Industrial Development," 50. On pages 50-51 Johnson cites a study by Neal G. Lineback which also is applicable to the establishment of the rayon plants in Elizabethton. Lineback found in his study of low wage firms in Tennessee that these companies had a catalytic effect on industrial development by raising the skill levels of the population and introducing the labor force to factory employment. Lineback's work is "Low Wage Industrialization and Town Size in Rural Appalachia," *Southeastern Geographer*, 12(1972), 1-13. For information on the skill needed to make rayon see Blicksilver, "Man-Made Fibers," 23-24.

11. *American Bemberg Annual Report for Year Ending 1927* (hereafter cited as *Annual Report*), pp. 1-2; *Annual Report 1928*, p. 1.

12. On the 1929 strikes see Tippett, *When Southern Labor Stirs*, pp. 54-75; Hall, "Disorderly Women," 354-82; F. Ray Marshall, *Labor in the South* (Cambridge, MA: Harvard University Press, 1967), pp. 105-07; Irving Bernstein, *The Lean Years. A History of the American Worker 1920-1933* (New York: Da Capo Press, 1960), pp. 14-20; Hodges, "Great Textile Strike," 343-57; Sherwood Anderson, "Elizabethton," *Nation*, 128(May 1, 1929), pp. 526-27; Margaret Bowen, "10.64 a Week: Testimony by a Textile Striker at Elizabethton," *New Republic*, 59 (May 29, 1929), 41-43; E.J. Eberling, "Strikes Among Textile Workers in the Southern States," *Current History*, (30 June 1929), pp. 450-53; "Strike Closes Plant," *ES*. (March 14, 1929), p. 1; and "Strikers at Plant Form Local Union," *ES*, (March 14, 1929), p. 1.

13. Bemberg alone lost approximately 15,000 pounds of production per day for the duration of the strikes. While Bemberg earned a net profit of $619,153 for 1928, it lost $499,832 for 1929. See *Annual Report, 1928 and 1929*. For payroll and production figures through the depression years see Holly, "Elizabethton," pp. 232, 285. *Moody's Manual of Investments* (hereafter referred to as *Moody's*), 1930-39, provided comparative income statistics for American Bemberg and North American Rayon. The 1932 and 1933 Moody's did not list American Glanzstoff separately: for those years only statistics for Bemberg are available.

14. Holly, "Elizabethton," pp. 232, 285.

15. For Bemberg profits see *Annual Reports, 1929-39*. *Moody's* 1933-41 provides data on Bemberg and North American stock dividends. As mentioned, the 1932 and 1933 *Moody's* did not list American Glanzstoff separately: only Bemberg was listed for those years.

16. Holly, "Elizabethton," p. 151. Two articles in the *ES*, February 5, 1929, pp. 1 and 6, discuss WDC's activities, specifically, allegations that new employees were being forced to rent houses built by WDC.

    It appears that WDC in essence was succeeded by River View Realty Co., a subsidiary of Bemberg and North American. Bemberg owned one-third interest, while North American owned the balance. See *Moody's*, 1947, p. 687; and 1949, p. 2337.

17. *Moody's*, 1949, p. 2337-2338. The stock of Bemberg and Glanzstoff was transferred to AKU. See *Annual Report. Office of Alien Property. Department of Justice* (hereafter referred to as OAP Report). For Fiscal Year Ended June 30, 1948 (Washington, D.C.: House Document no. 89, 81st Congress, 1st Session, p. 35.)

18. Holly, "Elizabethton," pp. 137-38.

19. See Ibid, p. 156 for Elizabethton's population, 1890-1940, and p. 202 for retail sales in Elizabethton, 1931-47. Correlation coefficients were obtained through use of SPSSX "Pearson Correlation" program. Coefficients for retail sales, Carter County, and total rayon plant payrolls, 1931-47; and number employed at the plants and retail sales, Carter County, 1931-47, were .9919 and .9952 respectively.

20. *OAP* Report, pp. 34-37.

21. For the financial status of the plants see Ibid., pp. 37-39, and *Moody's*, 1949, pp. 2337-38. For numbers employed at the plants in 1949 consult *Directory of Tennessee Industries* (Tennessee State Planning Commission, 1949), p. 41. For a brief history of Beaunit see "Brief History of Beaunit Mills, Inc.," *Watauga Spinnerette*, 27(May 1950), pp. 12-13. The 1949 *Annual Report* for Beaunit details what types of rayon the plants produced.

22. Wright, *Old South. New South*, pp. 263-64.

23. Blicksilver, "Man-Made Fibers," 16-17.

24. *Beaunit Mills Annual Report for 1959* (hereafter cited as *Beaunit Annual Report*), pp. 6-8; *Beaunit Annual Report, 1956*, np.

25. Blicksilver, "Man-Made Fibers," 17; *Beaunit Annual Report, 1966*. p. 2; and *Moody's Public Utility Manual* (hereafter cited as *Moody's PUM*), pp. 1506, 1513.

26. *Beaunit Annual Report*, p. 2.

27. Ibid. Blicksilver, "Man-Made Fibers," 16-18, discusses trends in the synthetic fibers markets.

28. *Beaunit Annual Report, 1967*, p. 2, and *Moody's, 1968*, p. 742. For numbers employed at the plants from 1949 through 1967 see *Directory of Tennessee Industries* and *Tennessee Directory of Manufacturers* (Tennessee State Planning Commission).

29. For numbers employed in Carter County and Elizabethton, again consult *Directory of Tennessee Industries* and *Tennessee Directory of Manufacturers*.

30. On the sale of Bemberg and Beaunit see Joe Ledford, "Beaunit Sold; Most Operations to Continue," *Johnson City Press-Chronicle (JCPC)*, December 16, 1976, p. 1; "Fire Sad Ending for Story of Once Thriving Industry," *JCPC*, November 9, 1981, p. 6; *Moody's PUM*, 1977, p. 667 ("El Paso Company"); Ibid, 1976, p. 650 (also "El Paso Company." El Paso Natural Gas Co. had become a subsidiary of El Paso Co.); and "Beaunit Sold," *Wall St. Journal*, December 16, 1976, p. 4.

For information on North American becoming an ESOP company see *ES*, February 23, 1986, p. 1; and *NAR Spinnerette*, January 1987, pp. 1-3.

References to 1920s and 1930s *Elizabethton Star* articles were provided by Norma Thomas, Archivist, Archives of Appalachia, East Tennessee State University. The author thanks Ms. Thomas for her help.

INSTRUCTION AND PROFESSIONAL DEVELOPMENT
  Convenor: Phyllis Bickers
Community, Kinship and Communication: Teaching In Appalachia
  Ardeth M. Deay, West Virginia University
  Susan Day-Peroots, West Virginia University
Process Instruction in Appalachian Studies—A Case Example Using *Education in Appalachia's Central Highlands*
  Mark F. Sohn, Pikeville College
The "Si-Godlin" Language Arts Education of Appalachian Schools
  Thomas Cloer, Furman University
Student Paper Competition Winner

Process Instruction in Appalachian Studies: A Case Example Using Education in Appalachia's Central Highlands

by
Mark F. Sohn

Introduction

Education in Appalachia's Central Highlands is the result of a decade of concern about Appalachian studies at Pikeville College. The College started to consider its Appalachian mission ten years ago and with this book—to use a term from the conference theme—celebrates Appalachian studies. In particular, this book celebrates student research. It is a culmination of research papers from a Pikeville College course, Appalachian Education. It is a historical and current analysis of education in the central highlands of Appalachia—Eastern Kentucky, southern West Virginia and the western tip of Virginia.

This paper will present the theory of education that supports the development of a cognitive-process approach to Appalachian studies. It will then present the book as a case example. A focus of the paper will be on research findings.

There are two styles of education: process and product. With product instruction, the teacher pursues a specific preplanned course. Educational outcomes are well-known in advance and the student may follow a rigid path to achieve course or behavorial objectives. Outcomes are measured against pre-established objectives. The student participates in product instruction by attempting to meet teacher-established expectations.

Process instruction, the focus of this paper, requires creative, involved and critical participation on the part of the student. Learning outcomes are less specific. Learning processes, however, are known in advance, tending to include research, discovery, discussion, writing and experimentation. The student acts on his environment and gets involved with content in a personal way. The student's environment and the student's objectives are central to the educational experience. The student may become physically, socially and emotionally involved in the subject matter. None of this is new— educators and theorists have debated process and product instruction since the beginning of time. Here is a review of the theory.

Educational theorists Piaget, Montessori, Bruner and Asubal are cognitive process theorists. The application of process instruction to Appalachian studies is obvious. But for those teachers who like to work from a textbook or for those teachers who like to know in advance the learning outcomes, any movement from a prescribed course of instruction is difficult. If, on the other hand, one applies Carl Rogers' concept of "teacher as facilitator," then student interests become central to the educational process and the environment, the community, the family, the local church, all become sources of information. The teacher is no longer an expert, but a consultant, an interested party.

Piagetian theory suggests that the student should be active in manipulating materials and constructing ideas. Experience, says Piaget, facilitates growth. Appalachian topics and people are ideal for the student to interview, photograph, experience and write about. The interview itself offers a trial and error forum from which students can demonstrate their skills and at the same time, gather information in an order and form which they direct. The learner becomes an inquirer, a doer, a maker, a force in the world. What impact my students have had!

For Jerome Bruner, educational theorist, the ability to conceptualize, that is, to perceive and understand relationships, is paramount. In Appalachian studies, driving down the road, going to the library, checking a church record book, studying school annuals or yearbooks, all of these things force the student to see the relationships in their community. Ask them to relate their subject to local, state or national developments and you have a mind task. Bruner's discovery learning can be used as a curriculum development guide. Here the teacher and the student together arrange questions, resources and experiences that lead to active information processing. Appalachian studies provides an ideal forum for this learning process.

Bruner breaks learning into three parts. He calls them the enactive, iconic and symbolic modes. Appalachian studies is a forum for learning in each of these modes. The enactive mode involves actions and events. The iconic mode occurs when the student uses images and pictures to represent the world. These images and pictures are in the mind and without action. In the symbolic mode, the student uses words or writing to express those thoughts developed in the enactive mode. As the growth of feelings, beliefs and values are a goal, this involved process is a growth medium. We teach Appalachian studies to teach pride, love and affection. Do this with enactive, iconic and symbolic modes.

For David Asubal, learning must be "meaningful learning." Learning becomes meaningful with the use of advance organizers and integrative reconciliation. These concepts are easily applied to Appalachian studies. The advance organizer is the child's or student's background—his home, his community, his family, his church. These points of reference help build a structure for learning. These advance organizers are introductory statements. When the data are gathered, then the student can be encouraged to move to a higher level called integrative reconciliation. Here the student takes the virgin bits of information and puts them together. Data are compared, contrasted, integrated and reconciled. Conclusions and evaluations are drawn. Predictions are developed. This, of course, requires the cognitive ability Piaget calls formal operations. And while Asubal's theories are normally applied to the junior high and high school levels, those of Maria Montessori are applied to preschoolers, but not limited to that category.

Maria Montessori is a process instruction-oriented theorist because she recognizes sensitive periods, uses didactic materials and provides for developmental needs, such as orderliness. Her concepts merit application to junior high, high school or college Appalachian studies programs, specifically, sensitive periods for the individual and for the culture. It suggests that both individuals and cultures have particular times at which they are most suited for advancement, study and evaluation which lead to progress . In Appalachian studies, one uses artifacts—a la Montessori, these are didactic materials—to involve students physically in their culture.

In my course, I have an artifacts night: Each student brings an object, an Appalachian object, to share with the class. Another process-oriented technique, old as the hills, is the Appalachian dinner. Here students act on their heritage, their health and their environment by preparing an Appalachian dish, writing the recipe and sharing the results with the class. A third and more scholarly approach to process instruction in Appalachian studies is the term paper.

With ten short papers, all part of one long paper, students in Appalachian Education are guided through the term paper ethnographic research process. The ten short papers that lead up to one long paper are as follows: (1) a sample paper, a short two-page example of a paper on Appalachian studies, (2) interview questions, ten prepared questions, (3) a written interview taken from either a tape recording or notes of an interview, (4) topic and outline, ten headings, topic and outline for the final paper, (5) source list, name, phone number, address of interview subjects, must list primary sources and secondary sources, (6) five sample notecards, (7) ten sample footnotes, (8) appendix material, photos, graphs-fully labeled and numbered, (9) rough draft of final paper, (10) peer review. The peer review includes both a self-evaluation of the paper and a peer evaluation. These ten papers guide the students through the term paper writing process. This approach calls the student into personal reflection on his past and future.

Education in Appalachia's Central Highlands was researched and written using this approach. This textbook is in keeping with the concept of process instruction because it is incomplete and in progress. It will always be in progress because as students add to it, they become a part of it. While it is complete, it is not complete: Each chapter has questions for further research and study . Students continue the process of collecting and sharing the Appalachian experience through their own term papers, their interviews and their peer reviews. The experience is didactic, interactive and integrative. It often compares Appalachian and non-Appalachian, today's experience with yesterday's, good with bad, urban with rural and rich with poor. Education in Appalachia's Central Highlands is a process text, incomplete and student-owned. Each chapter has questions to answer, terms to define, photos to take, poems to write, etc. Student-taken photos and student-written poetry illustrate the chapters.

Chapels in the Mountains

by
Marc Sherrod

During the first half of the 20th Century, the Presbyterian Church recognized the Appalachian region as fertile ground and as a worthy opportunity for sharing the Gospel with people in need of salvation. The establishment of churches for evangelism, schools for education, hospitals for healing, and orphanages for the homeless represented a growing Presbyterian influence and outreach in the region. In the Presbytery of Holston,[1] which included four counties in western North Carolina and twelve counties in eastern Tennessee, this influence and outreach developed in large part out of the Presbytery's participation in the denomination-wide Home Missions movement.

In 1915, the General Assembly of the Presbyterian Church in the United States formed the Synod of Appalachia.[2] Not long after this, the concept of Home Missions had established itself within the denomination as a legitimate method for sharing the Gospel, especially to disadvantaged and to unreached people throughout the South and throughout the Appalachian region. During this portion of its history, missions were either "Foreign" or "Home" for the Presbyterian Church. The potential of Appalachia as a "great home mission field" helped to justify the creation of the Appalachian Synod, for the new Synod "would develop a deeper interest for missions on the part of the mountain people by putting responsibility upon them."[3] Both before and with the formation of this new Synod, the Presbyterian Church came to regard Appalachia as a ripe field, ready for the harvest. The denomination's Home Missions philosophy, then, became the principal means by which such a harvest would occur.

The Home Missions movement in Holston Presbytery focused on three areas of Christian concern: evangelism, education and equipment.[4] While the desire to bring about the salvation of souls remained a heavy emphasis of the Presbytery, so also did the Presbytery and its member churches seek to educate and to equip the people for engaging in the tasks of kingdom living. The establishment of schools and the sharing of material and monetary resources with people in the region fostered a unique Presbyterian presence which sought to minister to the whole person—mind, body, and spirit.

One of the primary results of the Home Missions movement and its efforts at evangelism, education, and equipment in Holston Presbytery was the development and sponsorship by local churches of a chapel ministry. These chapels also known as Sunday School outposts, preaching stations or preaching points, mission schools or mission churches—became integrally identified with the success of Home Missions in the Presbytery. As a microcosm for the entire Home Missions movement within the Presbytery, the concept of chapel ministries sought to combine attempts to win souls for Christ with the desire to provide both educational opportunities and the necessary funds so that the local people might erect and maintain a physical facility for worship and for educational purposes.

Essentially, the chapel was intended as an extension of the home or sponsoring church. Churches shared ministers and/or Sunday school workers with the chapel or chapels, and the home church governing body (the session) exercised oversight, supervision and leadership of the life and work at the chapel. People who attended a chapel were enrolled as members of the home church; the session, at least theoretically, shouldered primary responsibility for determining the nature and function of ministry at the chapel. While folks at the chapel maintained a separate identity from their fellow members at the church, this identity was simultaneously linked to the sponsoring congregation even as a child relates to his/her parent.

Chapels appeared on the scene in Holston Presbytery during a time when transportation and communication in the region were limited, a reality which often necessitated that much religious and social activity center within the local community. Furthermore, these chapels helped to provide a Christian environment and a Presbyterian presence in some rather isolated and self-contained communities. The establishment of chapel ministries by a home congregation also revealed a unique understanding for how church growth could occur. One common strategy for church growth in other denominations has been to divide the membership of a local church and then to initiate a separate congregation. This second congregation would have no direct relationship to the original church. Presbyterians, however, in the first half of the 20th Century utilized the chapel ministry as a way to subsidize financially and to encourage grass roots support and participation in an unreached community. By employing this strategy for church growth, the home congregation could provide direct supervision and leadership for the new, developing ministry at the chapel.

By 1926 in Avery County, North Carolina, four Presbyterian Churches had established chapel outpost ministries: the Banner Elk Presbyterian Church with a chapel later called Arbordale; the Pineola Presbyterian Church with a chapel in Linville; the Plumtree Presbyterian Church with four chapels — Slippery Hill, Buck Hill, Powder Mill, and Three Mile; and the Newland Presbyterian Church with the Blevins Creek Chapel and the Smokey Chapel. (Around 1945, the Fletcher's Chapel would be added as an outpost ministry of the Newland Church.) The chapels sponsored by all four of these churches rested within approximately a five mile radius of the home congregation. Today, the Arbordale Chapel of the Banner Elk Church is an independent Presbyterian congregation; the Livnille Chapel of the Pineola Church is no longer active; the Plumtree Church joined another Presbyterian denomination and the only chapel presently active is the Buckhill Church;[5] the Blevins Creek Chapel of the Newland Church is an independent church (the Blevins Creek Community Chapel), but it is no longer affiliated with the Presbyterian church; the former Smokey Chapel is now the Church of the Savior, a Lutheran-Episcopal Fellowship; the Fletcher's Chapel remains under the oversight of the Newland Church.

The history and current status of these chapels in Avery County is in large measure a commentary on the work of the Home Missions Committee of Holston Presbytery and on its efforts in working with those churches under its jurisdiction.

An examination of the chapel ministries sponsored by the Newland Presbyterian Church will be an attempt to address some of the following issues: Did Holston Presbytery's view of Home Missions change as changes such as improved roads and communications occurred within the bounds of Presbytery? Did the home church provide adequate oversight and supervision of these chapels? Did the theology and practice of the Home Missions movement encourage and instill a desire among the folk attending the chapels eventually to become self-supporting churches? Did the Christian influence and Presbyterian presence originally sought measure up to the expectations, hopes and prayers of the local churches involved and of the Presbytery?

Minutes of the Holston Presbytery meetings from 1920-1958 indicate a strong zeal for evangelistic efforts to carry the Gospel to unreached people living in the backyard of Presbyterian churches. A Presbytery staff person, usually referred to as the Home Mission Superintendent,[6] supervised the work of Sunday School and chapel extension. The report of the Home Mission Committee at the April 1, 1929 meeting of the Presbytery at First Presbyterian Church, Johnson City points to the evangelistic flavor of the committee's labors:

> Within the bounds of Presbytery, there are between 10,000 and 150,000 souls having reached the age of responsibility, and yet without Christ...Their souls are precious and the Master wants to win them everyone...Souls are hungry for the bread of life... During the past five years the country and mountain churches and missions to which your committee has contributed some aid have made some remarkable advances. Five churches have been built, three manses have been provided in fields which had no manse, three teachers' cottages have been built, and three chapels have been provided...A number of new Sunday Schools have been organized, others have been greatly increased in enrollment and attendance; at present the enrollment in this group of churches and missions is about double that of their church membership. Five years ago there were no daily vacation Bible schools held in the Presbytery; last summer more than 25 such were held with a total

enrollment of more than 1,500.... Looking backward, we are impressed with the fact that these five years have been fruitful years in soul-winning in this group of churches and missions. In the group as a whole there were less than 2,000 members at the beginning of this period. During these five years more than 1,000 members have been received on profession of faith and nearly half as many by letter.... this five year period has seen many changes at Banner Elk, which has been fittingly called by someone, the hub of the home mission work of Holston Presbytery...

The General Assembly of the Presbyterian Church also had a Home Mission Committee. In its report of 1931 to the Presbytery, this committee listed 310 outposts and unorganized preaching points [7] in existence across the denomination. In 1940, the Home Mission Committee of the Presbytery reported: "We have not reached the multitudes in our own Presbytery. The population of the 16 counties within the bounds of our Presbytery is approximately 350,000. The membership of all our churches is less than 8,000, and the Sunday School enrollment, is less than 10,000.[8] And then in 1955:

Our Committee is proud of the aggressive Home Mission spirit in most of the congregations. This is shown by increases in professions of faith, in giving and building programs.... The Committee assisted in the support of twelve pastors, who preached in thirty churches and chapels. In almost every case the pastor has more to do than is possible for one man to get done.... the brightest prospects for the expansion of our Home Mission work in the Presbytery are through the organization of outpost Sunday Schools... If the local churches will organize and provide voluntary workers for these Sunday Schools, the Home Mission Committee will assist in building chapels, and will take over some of the support of the work when it becomes an organized church.[9]

During this same 40 year period of successful Home Mission efforts for the Presbytery, the Newland Presbyterian Church also demonstrated remarkable growth. Constituted a church by action of a commission appointed by Holston Presbytery on August 12, 1917, the Newland Presbyterian Church itself was an "outpost" ministry, a new church development begun shortly after Avery County became the 100th North Carolina county in 1911. Newland was named the county seat and immediately Reverend Edgar Tufts [10] of Banner Elk and others made plans to erect a Presbyterian Church opposite the county courthouse of the town square. Beginning with 26 charter members, the Newland Church quickly grew to 66 on the Communicants Roll and 92 on the Sabbath School enrollment by 1929. By 1940, the membership roll included 160 people with 145 on the Sunday School roll and in 1951, 214 on the membership roll with no indication of the number on the Sunday School roll. [11]

After nine years of existence as an organized church, the Newland congregation and its session found themselves the overseer of two chapel outpost ministries — one in the Blevins Creek community and the other just outside of Newland in the Smokey Valley.

The Blevins Creek Chapel

As with the Newland Presbyterian Church, the Blevins Creek Chapel was in part established through the pioneering evangelistic work of Reverend Edgar Tufts of Banner Elk. (Blevins Creek is located about mid-way between Newland and Banner Elk.) The original building was erected around 1914 with local people in the Blevins Creek community providing the labor and materials. Prior to 1914, Mr. Hiram Brooks expressed concern about the destitute condition of the Blevins Creek area to Reverend Tufts. Although he had many ministerial obligations in several places in Avery and Watauga Counties, Reverend Tufts tried to preach at Blevins Creek once per month. After two years, Mr. Brooks left the area and Mr. and Mrs. R.E. Piercy, Sunday School extension workers affiliated with the Committee for Religious Education of Richmond, Virginia took over the Sunday School ministry at Blevins Creek. Actively involved with the Sunday School programs at Blevins Creek, Smokey and the Newland Church, Mr. Piercy labored for over 15 years as a Sunday School extension worker in Avery County. [12] He served as an elder in the Crossnore Church and later was elected to that same office at Newland.

The first mention of the Blevins Creek Chapel in the sessional records of the Newland Presbyterian Church occurs on August 26, 1917. "The session met at Blevins Creek School-house at 4:30 pm at close of service." Mr. Donald Brown was received as a member upon reaffirmation of faith. Although this meeting at Blevins Creek occurred two weeks after the Newland Church was constituted, it would be 22 years later on March 26, 1939 before the session again would meet at Blevins Creek.

At a meeting of Holston Presbytery held at Shull's Mill, North Carolina (September 13, 1921), a petition for organization as a church was received from the Blevins Creek outpost. The action of the Presbytery on this petition is unclear, though presumably the petition was either denied or the members who attended the chapel never acted upon their request since Blevins Creek remained a chapel well into the 1980s.

A school, in addition to a Sunday School, had apparently been established by 1917 at Blevins Creek, with Mr. and Mrs. Piercy serving as teachers. Mr. Walter Vance, whose wife's family (Mr. Morris Lee) donated the land for the Blevins Creek Chapel, remembers that from the outset education went hand in hand with church work: "the school's purpose was to educate people and to educate them towards Christ... to provide a school and a Christian atmosphere for the people of the Blevins Creek area."[13] Public education was only offered for three months out of the year, so the school at Blevins Creek supplemented apparently the 'secular' education of local youngsters while offering opportunities to share the Gospel and to provide instruction in the Christian faith. Mr. Vance and his wife recall hearing about the influence of Mormon missionary teams who passed through the area and they think that perhaps this Mormon presence had something to do with the desire of the Blevins Creek residents to erect a school/church building in their community.

Sometime around 1951, a new building was constructed at Blevins Creek. The cost was $3,100 with a contribution of $600 received from the Home Mission Committee of Holston Presbytery. The session of the Newland Church and the Presbytery were actively involved in seeking financial support for the building of this new facility. At a session meeting on September 5, 1952, appreciation was expressed to the Calvary Presbyterian Church of Johnson City and to Mr. Beeson, a Presbyterian layman, architect and chairman of the Home Mission Committee. They had been "instrumental in the physical and spiritual support given the Newland Presbyterian Church on building of new Blevins Creek Chapel."

Despite the clear interest shown in this new building project, from 1917 till 1951, session minutes reveal only occasional references to the work transpiring at Blevins Creek. References include new member receptions, the need for the church to provide adequate insurance coverage, and enrollments in Sunday School and in Vacation Bible School. On May 1, 1950, the session appointed Mr. Morris Lee as the Sunday School Superintendent at Blevins Creek. Other than Mr. Piercy, there is no indication that elders from the Newland Church had direct involvement in the ministry at this chapel. According to his daughter Mrs. Vance, Mr. Lee was elected an elder but his name does not appear at the outset of any session meeting when members in attendance were listed.

On February 7, 1956, the clerk of session "was asked to write the Crossnore Church and Presbytery concerning the possibility of Crossnore assuming Blevins Creek as a chapel in the Crossnore field." It was reported on March 25 of that same year that "the Crossnore session voted to accept Blevins Creek as a part of the Crossnore Church and to sponsor services and request that all members join the Crossnore Church." While it is likely that Presbytery's Home Mission Committee agreed to this transfer, there is not any evidence of protest from any party concerned, including the folks at the Blevins Creek Chapel.

Prior to the transfer of the chapel to the oversight and care of the Crossnore Church, ministers of the Newland Church preached at Blevins Creek on a somewhat irregular basis — sometimes on Saturday night, sometimes on Sunday afternoon or Sunday night. However, Mr. and Mrs. Vance recall with fondness many of the "preachers" who served the field at Blevins Creek, especially Reverend Frank Camp and his wife. During Reverend

Camp's tenure,[14] he provided the Sunday School literature for the chapel, apparently purchasing it himself. Such generosity was deeply appreciated by the folks at Blevins Creek, for it was a time, according to Mr. Vance, when we might receive "15¢— 2¢ in the offering plate." It was a "good thing that they would help us — otherwise we never would have made it on our own without the support of Newland."

The Smokey Chapel

In some ways the history of the Smokey Chapel parallels that of the Blevins Creek Chapel. The Smokey Chapel began in a "little shack of a church," according to Mrs. Viola Oaks, across the road from its present location about two miles outside of Newland on the 'Smokey straight.' In either 1923 or 1924, the building was dedicated.[15]

Reverend D.B. McLaughlin, pastor of the Newland Church from 1921-1926, was instrumental in helping to get the Smokey Chapel established. At one point in its history, the chapel was named Mac's (or Max's) chapel in honor of Reverend McLaughlin, but through common use the title Smokey Chapel came to be the accepted name. The Chapel is located in the Smokey Valley, hence the name. Reverend McLaughlin had friends in Johnson City who donated some of the materials for the chapel. Parts of an old church in Pineola were also used along with the labor of local people.[16]

The folks who attended the Smokey Chapel received the preaching services of the pastor at Newland about twice a month. Like Blevins Creek, the preaching schedule varied from minister to minister — sometimes on Saturday night, sometimes on Sunday morning, Sunday afternoon, or Sunday night. For a time while Reverend Camp was pastor, his wife led the Sunday School program at Smokey, perhaps in part at least, paralleling the role of Mr. and Mrs. Piercy at Blevins Creek. Though it is not clear precisely how he did it, Mr. Piercy also played an instrumental role in helping to establish the Sunday School program at Smokey. Following the pastorate of Reverend Saunders who succeeded Reverend Camp, Mrs. Viola Oaks superintended the Sunday School at Smokey.

Around 1954, Mr. Oaks added on three Sunday School rooms to the original building. As with the Sunday School programs at the other chapels and at the Newland Church, numerical growth on the Sunday School rolls had been steadily increasing for a number of years. In large part through the efforts of Mr. D.R. Beeson of Johnson City, Holston Presbytery's Home Mission fund gave $5000.000 towards this building project. The money was channeled through the Newland session. For the most part during its history, however, financial resources were limited at the Smokey Chapel. According to Mr. Oaks, about "all we could swing were the expenses — oil, wood, electricity, Sunday School literature." There is no indication that anyone from the

Smokey Chapel was ever elected to the office of elder. As with the Blevins Creek Chapel, several session meetings were held at Smokey, primarily to receive new members. Evidently, elders also attended the chapel at Smokey in order to assist with the administration of the sacraments. The first mention of the Smokey Chapel in the session minutes relates to the reception of new members. On March 28, 1938, "the following were received into the church from Smokey Mission having been duly examined and baptized November 7, 1937, and expressing a desire to unite with our church." Interestingly, six months passed between the examination and baptism and the official reception and recognition of church membership. [17]

As spokespersons for their respective chapels, both the Vances and the Oaks indicated that there was a growing concern during the last decade or so of the chapels' relationship with the Newland Church that "a burden was being placed on the in-town church." About ten years after the Blevins Creek Chapel was "given" to the Crossnore Church for oversight and supervision, the Newland Church considered the possibility of selling the Smokey Chapel to one of several interested parties. In 1967, an agreement was reached with the Assembly of God for rental of the church, though Presbyterian services continued to be held there on an intermittent basis. On January 13, 1972 the following motion appeared in the session records:

> Motion was made and passed that every member of Smokey Chapel be notified that if support, interest, and attendance is [sic] not what it should be by March, preaching services will be discontinued and the situation will be reviewed by the session as to the possibility of closing the Sunday School program.

Concern again was expressed in April of 1975 about the "growing concern over the dormant state of the Smokey Chapel." On June 2, 1982, the building and property of the Smokey Chapel was deeded over to Mr. and Mrs. Theodore Oaks, with the stipulation that should it ever cease to be a church, that the trustees of the Presbytery of Concord would have first option at purchasing it. [18] Soon afterwards, the Smokey Chapel became a Lutheran congregation under the leadership of Reverend O.T. McRee.

The Fletcher's Chapel

The Fletcher's Chapel (also known as "The Chapel" or as "the Church on Cow Camp Road") is located two miles from the Newland Presbyterian Church. It is named after Mr. Ragland Fletcher, a former member of the Newland Church and now a retired Presbyterian minister. Prior to WWII and before his ordination, Mr. Fletcher was an active Sunday School worker in that area of Avery County known as "Cow Camp," and he taught an afternoon Sunday school class in various people's homes from 1939-1943. Shortly after the close of WWII, the present building was constructed with labor and materials supplied by folks in the local community. Preaching services were held fairly regularly (about twice a month), the pastor often alternating Sundays between Smokey Chapel and Fletcher's Chapel.

According to the session meeting on January 12, 1939 "R.E. Piercy, Ronald Hughes and Ragland Fletcher were appointed as trustees of the church proposed at Cow Camp." The proposed church, later named after Mr. Fletcher, does not appear again in session minutes until June of 1949; "Reverend Crinkley discussed in detail the fine work being done in the three outposts, with respect to both church and Sunday School." Up until 1976, the pattern of sessional leadership and oversight for Fletcher's Chapel followed the course set at Blevins Creek and Smokey. Aside from Sunday School provided by Mr. Fletcher and an occasional session meeting at the Cow Camp Chapel to receive new members, there is no indication that any substantial direction was given to this outpost ministry by the elders of the Newland Church.

Since 1976, however, at least one elder from Fletcher's Chapel has served on the session of the Newland Church. Mr. Ben Wise and Mrs. Gloria Wise presently serve on the session; Mr. Roger Wise, son of Ben Wise, served from 1976-1984. An annual Vacation Bible School is held jointly by Newland Church and Fletcher's Chapel, and for the past two years the chapel has hosted the event. Opportunities for mutual participation and fellowship between folks at the church and the chapel are offered, but usually the attendance at these events depends on the place — church, chapel or neutral site. Worship services are held each Sunday morning at the Chapel followed by Sunday School.

Although it can be argued that Fletcher's Chapel did not really participate in the Presbyterian form of government until some of its "members" began serving as elders in 1976, there remained something attractive and unique about Presbyterian theology and practice. Reverend Fletcher commented, "I was always struck that they wanted a Presbyterian Church . . . instead of a Baptist or Holiness type of church . . . they seemed to want more of an intellectual rather than an emotional approach to religion."

Conclusions

The 60 year history of chapel oversight by the Newland Presbyterian Church is clouded by the apparent lack of continuous and significant leadership given to these three chapels. Neither the Home Mission Committee of the Presbytery nor the elders of the Newland Church attempted to cultivate leadership qualities within folks attending these chapels, at least not until 1976. The relationships between the "parent" church and its "daughter" chapels were maintained primarily through a ministerial presence and through the faithful labors of Sunday School extension workers such as Mr. Piercy and Mr. Fletcher. On one occasion (October 2, 1968) the session appointed a special committee to "review the Presbyterian Church and chapel situation in Avery County." The Women of the Church, a Presbyterian Women's organization at Newland, sometimes studied materials produced by the Home Mission Committee of the Presbytery or of the General Assembly as a way to inform themselves about the work transpiring with these outpost ministries. However, such attempts at increased understanding were few and far between.

The Home Mission Committee of Holston Presbytery ceased to exist in 1956 and its work was assumed under the new name, Church Extension Committee. While the Presbytery records do not address the specifics of this change, this shift in emphasis from Home Mission to Church Extension signaled the closing of the "chapel outpost" movement as a way to "evangelize, educate and equip." Perhaps the Presbytery realized the peculiar pressures placed on a sponsoring church which found it difficult to oversee one or more chapel ministries.

The parent/child relationship encouraged by the creation of chapel ministries fostered an unhealthy dependence by the "child-chapel" on the "parent-church." Some chapels, such as the Arbordale chapels of the Banner Elk Church, eventually became a self-supporting congregation. However, most of the chapels in Avery County, including those sponsored by the Newland Church, never reached an independent status — at least as a Presbyterian congregation. In all likelihood, they were never offered the opportunity to become self-sufficient, probably because of their relatively small size and the lack of potential for significant numerical growth in their respective communities.

Evidently, there was a desire for a Presbyterian presence and influence among the folks within whose communities these chapels were started. However, recent history indicates that both the Smokey and Blevins Creek Chapels are no longer affiliated with the Presbyterian Church and people who traditionally attended these chapels continue to do so even after the chapel is no longer tied to a Presbyterian denomination. The principal loyalty appears to be to the chapel itself and not to the sponsoring church or denomination. Each of these three chapels has drawn its membership from families within the local, geographically specific neighborhood. While, as Reverend Fletcher notes, there is something very attractive about Presbyterianism to the people at Cow Camp, Fletcher's Chapel remains largely a family chapel and its identity is less associated with Presbyterianism than it is as, simply "the Chapel."

The Fletcher's Chapel and possibly the other two former Presbyterian Chapels as well, suffers from a split over rural and town values. The Chapel is a country/rural congregation with an informal and relaxed understanding of what the church should be about. The church, on the other hand, serves people who come from a wider diversity of backgrounds and whose formal education levels are generally higher than those of people attending the chapel. The nature and function of ministry at the church engenders greater structure and formality within those who share in the life of its ministry. This deeply ingrained mindset of a split over rural/town values and ways of engaging in kingdom work seems to limit the future possibilities for togetherness and mutual growth between folks at the chapel and folks at the church.

NOTES

1. The Presbyterian Church operates under a representative from the church government. There are four governing bodies: 1) the *Session*, composed of elders elected by the people, is the governing body for the local church; 2) the *Presbytery*, a collection of Presbyterian churches in a certain geographical area, exercises oversight of member churches within its boundaries; 3) the *Synod* is a regional unit composed of a collection of Presbyteries; and 4) the *General Assembly* is the national governing body for the entire denomination.

2. The Presbyterian Church in the United States, also known as the southern Presbyterian Church, split from the Presbyterian Church in 1861. The Synod of Appalachia covered the mountainous sections of four states: North Carolina, Tennessee, Virginia and Kentucky. The Synod was dissolved by action of the General Assembly in 1971 (?).

3. *Highways and Byways of Appalachia*, E.M. Craig, ed., Kingsport Press: Kingsport, Tennessee, 1927, p. 14.

4. "Our Jerusalem," Walter Keys, ed., published by the Home Mission Committee of Holston Presbytery, 1926, p. 5.

5. Less than a decade ago the Plumtree Church joined the Evangelical Presbyterian Church, a denomination which split off from the former PCUS (now PCUSA following reunion of the northern and southern branches in 1983). The Buckhill Chapel (now a church) followed the parent Plumtree congregation in leaving the denomination. Present status of the other three chapels is unknown. The Frank Presbyterian Church, now a member church of the Presbyterian Church in America, yet another splinter group, possibly also began as an outpost ministry of the Plumtree Church.

6. Holston Presbytery meeting at the Newport Presbyterian Church in Newport, Tennessee, April 12, 1937. Here, for the first and possibly only time, the head of the Home Mission Committee is referred to as an Evangelist-Superintendant.

7. Holston Presbytery meeting at the First Presbyterian Church of Jefferson City, Tennessee, April 20, 1931, i.e. the Assembly's Home Mission report.

8. Holston Presbytery meeting at the Micaville Presbyterian Church of Micaville, North Carolina, April 22, 1940. Interestingly, no mention in this report is made of Christians belonging to other denominations. The implication is that the Presbyterian Church is the only way!

9. Holston Presbytery meeting at Cold Spring Presbyterian Church of Bristol, Tennessee, January 18, 1955.

10. Edgar Tufts was a prolific Presbyterian minister who helped start numerous churches and other Christian agencies in the Banner Elk area. The present day Edgar Tufts Memorial Association includes Lees-McRae College, Cannon Memorial Hospital and Grandfather Home for Children.

11. It is difficult to determine how many if any of the members reported by the church actually attended one of the chapels. Sometime around 1940 or so, it appears that the session began to include as members folks in attendance at the chapels. However, since the registers were kept by hand and a form of short-hand was utilized, such claims are difficult to document.

12. See Women of the Church history as the history describes Mr. Piercy (no page numbers).

13. Interview with Mr. and Mrs. Walter Vance, November 10, 1986.

14. Reverend Frank Camp pastored the Newland field from August 21, 1927 until February 1, 1942. He was an evangelist, and one of the best loved ministers during the history of the church.

15. An addition has now been added to the unused old sanctuary. This new addition houses the sanctuary, fellowship hall, kitchen and church offices of the Church of the Savior, a Lutheran-Episcopal Fellowship.

16. Information supplied by Mr. Theodore Oaks, October 28, 1986.

17. Why did so much time pass between the baptism and the actual reception into church membership? Normally, at most a week or two might transpire between the action of the session in receiving a new member and the act of the church in affirming that personal decision for Christ in baptism.

18. The details on the controversy surrounding the transfer of the Smokey Chapel to the Lutheran Church are not clear. However, it apparently was a stormy time as personalities clashed and decisions were made about the Chapel's future.

Primary Sources

History of the Newland Presbyterian Church, ed. by Mrs. Frank Camp from 1917-1939 with an annual report submitted by the Women of the Church thereafter.

Interviews with the following:

1. Reverend Ernest Wilson, retired Presbyterian minister, affectionately known as "missionary to Holston Presbytery" (October 8, 1986).

2. Mr. and Mrs. Theodore Oaks of the Smokey Valley community (October 28, 1986).

3. Mr. and Mrs. Walter Vance of the Blevins Creek community (November 10, 1986).

4. Reverend Ragland Fletcher, retired Presbyterian minister from Newland and namesake of Fletcher's Chapel.

5. Mrs. Ellen Wise of the Cow Camp community (November 19, 1986).

Minutes of the Holston Presbytery, 1920-1958.

Minutes of the Session of the Newland Presbyterian Church, 1917-1986 (Books I-V).

Publications of the Home Mission Committee of Holston Presbytery: "The Holston Presbyterian," a newsletter of the committee from 1951-1958.

"Our Jerusalem," ed. by Walter Keys, Superintendent of the Home Mission Committee, 1926.

Secondary Sources

Highways and Byways of Appalachia, ed. by E.M. Craig, Kingsport Press: Kingsport, Tennessee, 1927.

COVERLET WEAVING
   Convenor: Tyler Blethen, Mountain Heritage Center, Western Carolina University
"New Threads In Old Patterns," Slide-tape presentation
   Jan Davidson, Mountain Heritage Center, Western Carolina University
Origins Of the Handicraft Revival In The Southern Mountains
   Curtis Wood, Mountain Heritage Center, Western Carolina University
   Joan Green, Special Collections, Western Carolina University
The Impact Of The 1895-1935 Craft Revival On Coverlet Weaving in Southern Appalachia
   Christopher Bobbitt, Indiana University

Origins of the Handicraft Revival in the Southern Mountains

by
Curtis Wood and Joan Greene

The origins of the Southern Appalachian handicraft revival lie in the late nineteenth and early twentieth centuries—a complex period in American history—a period that witnessed the many changes in lifestyle and attitude which accompanied an increasingly industrialized America. In the northeast families were leaving their farms and moving to the growing cities and towns; tenements continued to grow in cities such as New York, Chicago, and Boston as immigrants settled there. In many quarters there were growing concerns over the dehumanizing effects of the machine age and a desire to return to a simpler time, a time of a craftsman's pride in his workmanship. The progressive education movement was gaining momentum, and the followers of John Dewey expounded the theory that education is a social process and that the development of artistic abilities is a vital part of the educational process. The first colleges were being established for women, and as the role of women in American society continued to change, they became an effective force for social reform. The cities of the northeast, however, had no monopoly on change, and during the late nineteenth century events were transpiring which brought an era of rapid change to the Southern Appalachian mountains.[1]

Textile mills were moving south in search of cheap labor, and mountain families were moving into piedmont mill towns. The mountain regions were being opened by capitalists bent on exploiting the resources of the region. As improved transportation made remote areas more accessible, tourists were being drawn to the mountains by stories of the local color writers in newly-established magazines such as *Harper's and Scribner's*. Outsiders read stories of a land of haunting beauty inhabited by people who lacked educational advantages and the social amenities; people who were struggling to make a living on their mountainside farms; and people who, because of generations of mountain isolation, continued to live in the lifestyle of their ancestors. The culture of the southern mountain people was depicted as that of "pure" Americana, a simple, vital culture which had not been touched by the effects of industrialization but one which had been degraded by poverty. The result was the appearance in the mountain areas of social workers whose purpose was threefold: to provide education for mountain people; to encourage native handicrafts as a way of improving the mountain economy; and to nurture the traditional idealized rural life of (as William Frost said) "our contemporary ancestors." Many of the social workers were the products of the changing ideas and theories that were being advanced in the industrialized northeastern cities, and the implementation of those ideas and theories would result in the Southern Appalachian handicraft revival.[2]

The local color writers, however, had not prepared the newcomers for the realities of mountain life and culture, nor had they given them any insight into its traditions, complexities, or forms of expression. Instead, these potential social reformers were guided by perceptions of rural life, of honest labor, and a better world that were drawn from John Ruskin, William Morris, and their English and American followers and by the arts and crafts movement and social settlement experiences they had inspired. The ideas of Ruskin and Morris were in the mainstream of almost one hundred years of rebellion against the Industrial Revolution, and their teachings represent a late stage in this great social and cultural dialogue.

Both were influenced by Thomas Carlyle, Karl Marx, Robert Owen, Charles Dickens, and many others, but what was most original in the writings of Ruskin and Morris were their aesthetic concerns—their focus on the creativity and beauty of work and its social and cultural significance. Ruskin had condemned the dehumanizing aspects of the industrial age which alienated the worker from his products and drove beauty and meaning from work and life. Morris had turned these ideas into action and had become both a leader and an example. He wrote:

> We ought to get to understand the value of intelligent work, the work of men's hands guided by their brains, and to take that, though it be rough, rather than the unintelligent work of machines or slaves though it be delicate;...to have a high standard of excellence in ware and not accent make-shifts for the real thing....[3]

Morris set up craft workshops to revive dying crafts in an attempt to restore beauty and dignity to work. The arts and crafts movement with its love of that which was hand made and traditional was one result. Social settlements were another. In 1884 a handful of young Oxford University students opened a settlement house which they named Toynbee Hall in an industrial area of London. Their purpose was to serve the working poor by bringing beauty and learning into their lives, and Toynbee Hall served as an inspiration for the American social settlement movement.

Stanton Coit and Jane Addams were among the first Americans to visit Toynbee Hall and were instrumental in the transition of the settlement idea from England to America. In 1887 Coit established in New York's Lower East Side what has "usually been called the first American social settlement;" by 1889 Jane Addams's famous Hull House was operating in Chicago's East Side. As the English social settlement idea spread through the urban areas of northeastern cities, it was adapted to American needs and also became a decidedly women's movement.[4]

The many women who became involved in the social settlement movement were women of dedication, of strong beliefs. They were the first generation of college women in a time when the question of higher education for women was being vigorously debated, and perhaps they felt that they had to prove their right to a higher education by doing something important. Perhaps settlement work was an answer to the feelings of restlessness and uselessness they were experiencing in a changing society which still offered few careers to educated women. But whatever their motivation, they were a group of idealists who believed that settlement houses could help solve the problems of urban and industrial America, and they "organized America's first concerted attack on urban poverty."[5]

The workers who came to live in the settlement houses were a "diverse lot." They were engaged in various occupations— teachers, writers, artists— and while they were living at the settlement houses they "devoted their spare time to club and class work at the settlements." Nearly ninety percent had attended college; many had done graduate work and had studied abroad. They had studied economics, politics, and history; they "talked, argued, discussed. They debated Darwin's theories, talked about the role of women, a novel by Dickens, a Shakespearean play or one of Carlyle's books." They were young— the median age when they entered settlement work was twenty-five; they were enthusiastic; and they were committed to helping solve the "battle of the slums."[6]

The settlement houses were located in the middle of the worst neighborhoods, and their object was to educate the immigrants—not solely in the traditional sense of reading, writing, and arithmetic but as a means to social reform. As Lillian Wald, the founder of a settlement house on Henry Street in New York, stated: "Education in its broadest implication engages our attention first, last, and all the time." The American settlement movement, inspired by William Morris, immediately saw the value of crafts as a means to enrich the lives of the poor and to preserve the best of their traditional culture. Crafts classes served as a means of bringing the neighhborhood residents to the settlement houses where the educational process could be instituted; handicrafts were a source of social therapy as they brought people together, and they provided a source of pride as the workers were united with their finished products—products which were aesthetically pleasing. As Jane Addams said, "The aim of the settlement houses was 'to preserve and keep whatever of value [the immigrants' lives] contained,' and 'to bring them into contact with a better type of Americans.'"[7]

This paternalistic note of bringing the poor into contact with their "betters" was one characteristic of the settlement movement. Whether at Toynbee Hall, in the slums of northeastern cities, or in the communities of the Southern Appalachians, one of the primary goals of social workers was to "uplift" the natives by imbuing them with the social workers' values. One method of attaining this objective was through the use of handicrafts which, they believed, if pursued diligently became exercises in character-building. An echo of Ruskin encouraging women to weave and spin in order to develop moral fiber can be heard in a statement by a social worker in the southern mountains: "In the younger women who were learning to weave and keeping at it, I could see the growth of character."[8]

Another characteristic of the settlement movement was the attitude of social workers toward rural life. Although they never advocated abandoning urban life in favor of returning to a rural village existence, there was a powerful romanticism in their view of country living. Programs were instituted wherein children from the cities were sent to summer camps in the country where they could escape the problems of industrial America if only for a short time. There was also a growing sentiment to establish settlements in the rural areas of the country—in places where the social workers could bring educational advantages to the natives and where the natives could maintain their rural lifestyle. As the Southern Appalachian mountains came into public focus, this appeared to be the perfect setting for rural settlements. Here was an area of poverty-stricken, uneducated people who would benefit from social contacts; who were in need of education; and who lived simple lives that were untouched by industrialization. And as the settlement idea had made the transition from England to the cities in the northeast, the transition was made once again—this time to the Southern Appalachian mountains.[9]

In order that the social workers might provide the needed educational opportunities there was the necessity of bringing the natives together in the sparsely settled mountain communities. The obvious way to encourage gatherings was through crafts work, and as the settlement workers in the urban areas had encouraged the native crafts of the immigrants, the social workers in the southern mountains encouraged the native crafts of the mountaineers. Through handicrafts both idealistic and practical goals could be achieved because, as David Whisnant stated in his *All That Is Native and Fine*:

For reasons of their own, middle and upperclass people outside the region were acquiring a taste for traditional handicrafts. Mountaineers were among those who had the skills to satisfy that acquired taste and who were economically hard pressed enough to find the modest potential market attractive.

Thus, through the sale of crafts the economic base of the mountaineers could be improved. This would enable them to remain in the mountains rather than migrate to the mill towns which, to the social workers, embodied all the ills of an industrialized society.[10]

Settlement schools and handicraft centers began springing up independent of each other throughout the Southern Appalachians during the 1890s and early 1900s. Handicrafts such as weaving, basketry, quilting, rug making, woodcarving, pottery, and leather and metal work were promoted. Markets for the sale of these products were established through the handicraft centers: at Berea College and the Hindman Settlement School in Kentucky; at the Pi Beta Phi Settlement School in Tennessee; at the Tallulah Falls Industrial School and the Mount Berry School in Georgia; and in the Asheville area of western North Carolina. The earliest of the rural settlements, those in the Asheville area, were the Log Cabin Settlement established by Susan Chester Lyman in Buncombe County and Allanstand Cottage Industries established by Frances Goodrich in Madison County.[11]

Born in New York, Lyman was an 1888 graduate of Vassar College and had also been a resident at Hull House. She came to the Asheville area around 1892 hoping to establish a settlement school, and according to Frank Roberson whose mother attended the school, Lyman's earliest attempts included needlework sessions each morning for the girls in the neighborhood. From this beginning Susan Chester Lyman expanded her efforts to include a coverlet weaving program in 1895 for the ladies in the community. At first orders were sold to friends in the North, but by the late 1890s Lyman had made an arrangement with the Asheville Exchange for Women's Work to sell hand-woven goods on a commission basis at their salesroom on Court Square.[12]

Frances Goodrich, a social worker from New York, had been educated at the Yale Art School and in 1890 was assigned by the Presbyterian Home Missions to the station at Brittain's Cove in Buncombe County. There Goodrich discovered a tradition of coverlet weaving among the mountain women, and to her this suggested the idea of using weaving as a means of getting the women to come to the station and also as a way of sustaining their interest.

Goodrich proceeded in the typical settlement house manner and proposed a weaving project for the women who were meeting at the mission once a week. By 1895 she had determined that weaving was a skill which could provide added income for the mountain weavers as coverlets were sent North for sale. In 1897 Goodrich was transferred to Allanstand in Madison County where she continued to encourage hand weaving among the women of the area and where she organized the Allanstand Cottage Industries to handle the marketing of the woven products. In her book, *Mountain Homespun* which was published in 1931, Goodrich stated her purposes for encouraging the mountain handicrafts:

> ...to save the old arts from extinction; to give paying work to women too far from market to find it for themselves; and, more important than all, to bring interest into their lives, the joy of making useful and beautiful things.[13]

Frances Goodrich and Susan Chester Lyman were only two of the social workers who brought the settlement idea to the Southern Appalachians. During the early 1900s crafts centers continued to appear throughout the mountain region, and the Southern Appalachian handicraft revival was underway.

The social settlement movement which initiated the handicraft revival was many things to many people. It was a way of doing something useful and productive for a generation of college women who had not been accepted into a man's world of business and politics. It was a reaction against the effects of industrialization—a way of encouraging the continuation of a rustic lifestyle and a craftsman's pride in his workmanship. It was a way of bringing neighbors together in a social situation; a way of providing education in areas where schools were few and scattered; a way of adding cash to mountain family incomes. It was a preservation of old skills that were rapidly disappearing; it was a beginning.

NOTES

1. Oscar Handlin, *The Uprooted* (Boston: Little, Brown and Company, 1951), pp. 59, 133-135; Adolph E. Meyer, *The Development of Education in the Twentieth Century* (New York: Prentice-Hall, Inc., 1940), pp. 5-7; Edward H. Reisner, *The Evolution of the Common School* (New York: The Macmillan Company, 1930), p. 528; Allen F. Davis, *Life and Legend of Jane Addams* (New York: Oxford University Press, 1973), pp. 10-12.

2. Ronald D. Eller, *Miners, Millhands and Mountaineers Industrialization of the Appalachian South, 1880-1930* (Knoxville: The University of Tennessee Press, 1982), pp. 121-122, 125-126; Henry D. Shapiro, *Appalachia On Our Mind: The Southern Mountains and Mountaineers in the American Consciousness, 1870-1920* (Chapel Hill: The University of North Carolina Press, 1978), pp. 5-6, 115; Ina and John J. Van Noppen, *Western North Carolina Since the Civil War* (Boone: North Carolina: The Appalachian Consortium Press, 1973), pp. 355-358; Victoria Byerly, *Hard Times Cotton Mill Girls* (New York: Cornell University, 1986), pp. 11-12, 163; Ben F. Lemert, *The Cotton Textile Industry of the Southern Appalachian Piedmont* (Chapel Hill: The University of North Carolina Press, 1933), pp. 33, 48-49

3. Ian Hepburn, "The Craftsman and Social Conscience: William Morris," *Handwoven* (September/October 1984): 26.

4. Allen F. Davis, *Spearheads For Reform The Social Settlements and the Progressive Movement 1890-1914* (New York: Oxford University Press, 1967), pp. 8-11; David E. Whisnant, *All That Is Native & Fine* (Chapel Hill: The University of North Carolina Press, 1983), p. 21.

5. Cornelia Meigs, *What Makes a College? A History of Bryn Mawr* (New York: The Macmillan Company, 1956), pp. 2-3; Davis, *Spearheads for Reform*, pp. vii, 37-38.

6. Davis, *Spearheads For Reform*, pp. vii, 42-43; Davis, *Life and Legend*, p. 12; Meigs, p. 41.

7. Lillian D. Wald, *Windows on Henry Street* (Boston: Little, Brown and Company, 1934), p. 162; Charles A. and Mary R. Beard, *The Rise of American Civilization* (New York: The Macmillan Company, 1930), pp. 421-423; Whisnant, p. 45; Davis, *Spearheads For Reform*. p. vii.

8. Eileen Boris, *Art and Labor* (Philadelphia: Temple University Press, 1986), pp. 122-124; Frances Louisa Goodrich, *Mountain Homespun* (New Haven: Yale University Press, 1931), p. 25.

9. Davis, *Spearheads For Reform*, p. 23; Wald, pp. 158-159; Whisnant, p. 23.

10. Whisnant. p. 66.

11. Idyl Dial Gray, ed., *Azure-Lure* (Asheville, North Carolina: Advocate Publishing Co., 1924), n.p.; Marjorie Shearin, *Revival of Crafts in North Carolina*. Raleigh: North Carolina Agricultural Extension Service, 1966) pp. 8-9, 12; Allen H. Eaton, *Handicrafts of the Southern Highlands* (New York: Russell Sage Foundation, 1937), pp. 70-72; Max West, "Revival of Handicrafts in America," Bulletin of the Bureau of Labor, No. 55 (Washington, D.C.: Government Printing Office, 1904), pp. 1579-1580; Michael Frome, *Strangers in High Places* (Garden City, New York: Doubleday & Company, Inc., 1966), p. 235; "Educating the Boys and Girls of the Smokies," *The Great Smoky Mountains National Park* (Knoxville: Great Smoky Mountains Publishing Company, Inc., 1928), n.p.; Virginia Brackett Green, "Those Wonderful Years at the Settlement School," n.p., n.d., Courtesy of Arrowmont School, Gatlinburg, Tennessee.

12. Shapiro, p. 224; West, p. 1576; Interview, Frank Roberson, Asheville, North Carolina, 2 February 1987; "Questionnaire For Biographical Address Register," Vassar College, 19 May 1919; "Asheville Woman Disappears From Passenger Liner," Asheville Citizen, 25 January 1917, p. 1; James R. Reynolds to Jane Addams, 5 February 1893, in Jane Addams Papers, Peace Collection, Series 1, Supplement, Swathmore College.

13. Shapiro, p. 221; Shearin, p. 8; Goodrich, p. 25.

APPALACHIA: CONTRASTS AND SIMILARITIES
Convenor: Alvin E. Gerhardt, Rocky Mount Museum
Appalachia North
Ronald Sutherland, Universite, de Sherbrooke
Velma Jean Carter Sutherland, Sherbrooke, Quebec
A Look At Regional Patterns In The Southern Highlands
Paul E. Lovingood, Jr., University of South Carolina
Robert E. Reiman, Appalachian State University

A Look at Regional Patterns in the Southern Highlands

by
Paul E. Lovingood and Robert E. Reiman

Introduction

The Southern Highlands as defined here consists of 156 counties in the seven-state area of Georgia, Kentucky, North Carolina, South Carolina, Tennessee, and West Virginia. All but eight of the counties lie within the Appalachian Region as defined by the Appalachian Regional Commission, and the study area is generally referred to as The Appalachian Consortium Service Area (Figure 1).

Researchers from many disciplines in their study of the spatial form of human society have failed to recognize the existence of distinct areal units within a larger regional framework. In regional analysis it is necessary to establish some degree of regional distinction from the overwhelming mass of areal differences. In so doing one can understand a given area adequately, distinguish it from others and gain insight into the basic spatial organization in which people live and, in fact, the patterns which they have helped create. These patterns may be single-factor or multi-factor in character.

It is the purpose of this study, through the use of maps, to demonstrate the existence of many different regional patterns within the Southern Highlands. An attempt will be made to show the spatial patterns of various socioeconomic variables within the area, including but not limited to resources, agriculture, business, population and health care. This study will illustrate that analysis of socioeconomic data is not only incomplete but liable to serious error unless it is applied within a variety of regional frameworks.

FIGURE 1

Examples of Single-Factor Regions

<u>Farm Types</u>. Geographers and others have for many years attempted to delineate agricultural regions on the basis of production, sales, farm types, farm size, etc. As agriculture is basic to economic development, physical landscapes vary and man's adaptation to his environment changes through time and place; no two areas on the earth's surface are the same in terms of their agricultural patterns.

The map, Regions Based on Farm Types, shows five different regions in the Southern Highlands (Figure 2). Although tobacco and beef cattle can be found throughout the entire study area, certain regional specialties become obvious through an analysis of this map and its accompanying regional data (Table 1). The names of the regions were derived by using those farm types accounting for five percent or more of the total farms within a given region (Table 1).

Region 2, Beef/Tobacco/Cash Grain, contains the largest number of counties (85) and shows a dominance of beef cattle with tobacco ranking second and cash grain third. Region 3, Tobacco/Beef, is the second largest region with 51 counties. Tobacco is by far dominant in this region with beef cattle second. Region 1, Beef/Poultry, contains 13 counties most of which are in Georgia. Although beef cattle represents the highest percent of total farms in this region, there is a good balance between beef cattle and poultry production. Region 4, Beef/Tobacco/General Farming Livestock/Cash Grain/General Farming, Crops/Poultry, includes only four counties all located in the northern part of the study area. This represents an area of mixed

REGIONS BASED ON FARM TYPES - 1982

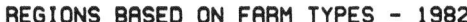

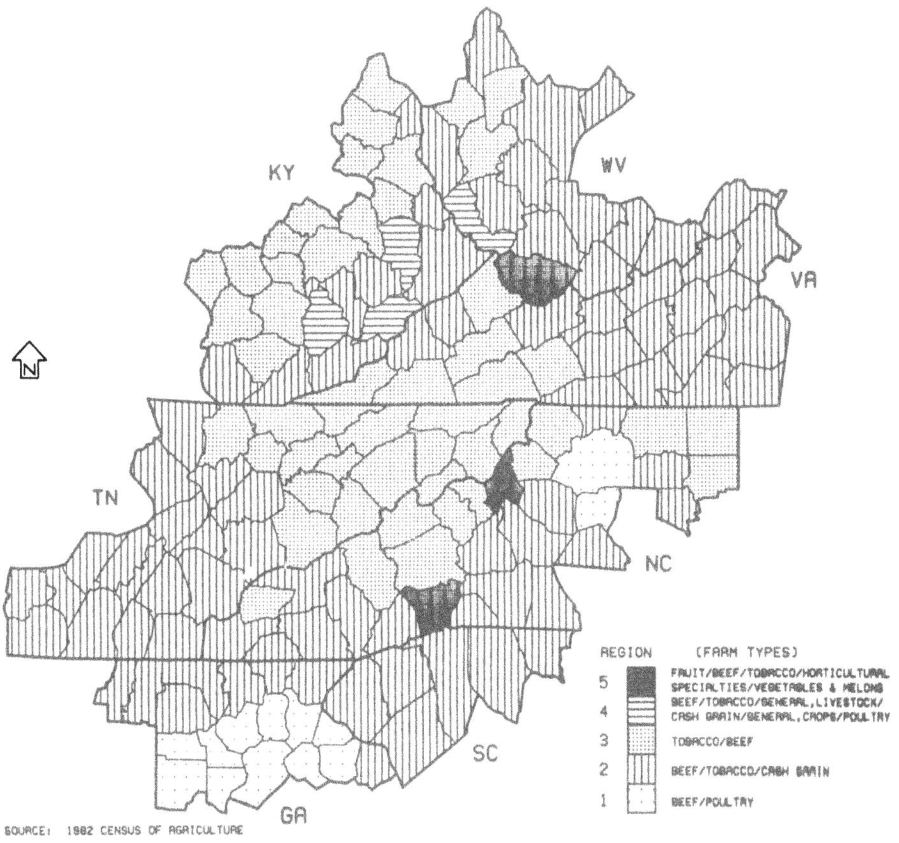

FIGURE 2.

agriculture with beef cattle, tobacco and general farming as the dominant activities. Region 5, Fruit/Beef/Tobacco/Horticultural Specialties/Vegetables and Melons, has only three counties which demonstrates a lack of "specialty farms" and a balanced agricultural economy throughout the study area.

<u>Business Employment</u>. Employment in the various businesses depicts the overall character of the economy of an area. The map, Regions Based on Employment in Each SIC Class as a Percent of Total Employment, shows five different regions in the Southern Highlands (Figure 3). There is considerable variation in the regional pattern throughout the study area (Table 2). Such variation should be expected because of the great range in both physical and cultural conditions in the area.

Region 1 consists of 58 counties and is located primarily in the southern part of the study area. In terms of employment (60 percent) it can truly be described as a manufacturing region. Retail trade and service employment

TABLE 1

PERCENT OF TOTAL FARMS BY FARM TYPE IN EACH REGION--1982

FARM TYPES	REGIONS				
	1	2	3	4	5
Cash Grain	3.6	6.5	1.4	9.0	2.0
Tobacco	2.7	10.8	65.4	13.1	10.3
Potatoes, Peanuts and Other Field Crops	2.7	4.3	1.6	4.1	3.1
Vegetables and Melons	1.1	2.1	0.5	3.2	8.8
Fruit and Tree Nuts	1.2	2.3	0.4	1.8	30.5
Horticultural Specialties	0.6	1.3	0.4	1.8	9.9
General, Primarily Crops	1.9	3.4	2.1	5.0	1.9
General, Primarily Livestock	1.0	1.2	1.0	10.4	1.0
Beef Cattle	42.9	51.1	20.0	30.3	22.1
Dairy	1.8	4.5	2.9	0.5	4.0
Poultry and Eggs	35.1	2.8	0.6	1.8	0.2
Animal Specialties	1.8	2.2	0.8	5.0	2.0
Region Size (Counties)	13	85	51	4	3

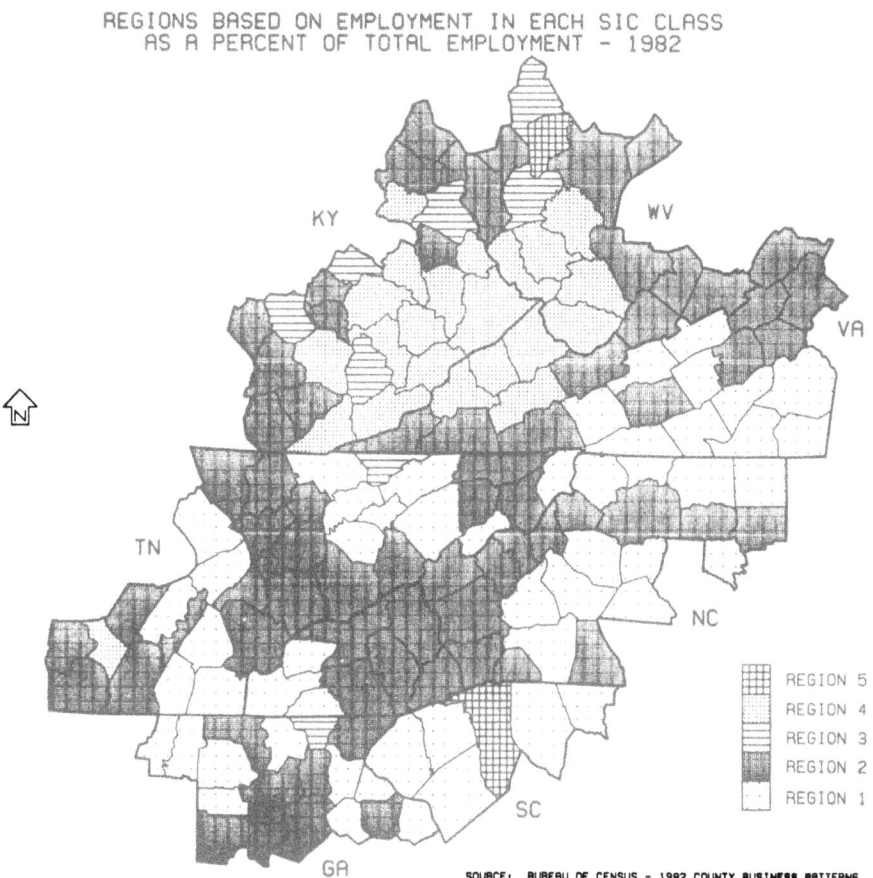

FIGURE 3.

support the manufactural employment. Region 2, the largest with 65 counties, is widely distributed throughout the study area. Employment here is more balanced with manufacturing, services and retail trade dominant but with important numbers in other categories. This could probably be described as the typical patterns of upland areas. Region 3 consists of only eight counties with over 50 percent of all employed persons engaged in tertiary activities. These are service centers but with significant employment in manufacturing. Region 4, 23 counties, is unique in that 50 percent of its employment is in the primary activity of mining. The retail trade and services employment in large part supports the mining activities. This traditional coal-mining region lacks diversity in terms of employment. Region 5 contains only two counties at op-

TABLE 2
PERCENT OF TOTAL EMPLOYMENT IN EACH REGION
BY SIC CLASS - 1982

SIC CLASS	REGIONS				
	1	2	3	4	5
Agricultural Services, Forestry and Fisheries	0.3	0.3	0.1	0.1	0.2
Mining	0.6	2.5	5.5	50.4	0.0
Contract Construction	3.8	5.3	3.5	2.1	32.0
Manufacturing	60.0	31.5	17.8	4.8	27.5
Transportation, Communication, Electric, Gas and Sanitary Services	3.0	5.5	18.5	4.0	3.0
Wholesale Trade	3.7	6.6	3.2	4.3	5.2
Retail Trade	14.6	20.8	24.9	16.9	13.4
Finance, Insurance and Real Estate	2.7	5.5	3.7	3.0	3.7
Services	11.5	21.9	22.1	14.3	15.0
Unclassified	0.1	0.1	0.7	0.3	0.0
Region Size (Counties)	58	65	8	23	2

posite "poles" in terms of their location and are anomalies in terms of their employment pattern. These are "high growth" areas as indicated by their significant employment in contract construction. In addition there is much diversity of employment which is characteristic of counties where large urban populations prevail.

Causes of Death. The map, Mortality Regions Based on Causes of Death, is used here to illustrate that regions may in fact exist with little or no significant differences between them (Figure 4). In the Southern Highlands there is little difference in the causes of death between sparsely populated rural counties as in Region 1 and the densely populated urban counties in Region 5 (Table 3). The percent of total deaths by cause for the most part does not vary more than about one percent between all five regions (Table 3). It is interesting to note that the percent of total deaths by cause, with one exception, is higher for all regions than the national average. The one exception is cirrhosis of the liver where three of the five regions are below the national average (Table 3). As would be expected the greatest number of deaths occur in those counties with higher populations (compare Figure 4 and Table 4).

TABLE 3
PERCENT OF TOTAL DEATHS BY CAUSE
PER REGION - 1980

Cause	\multicolumn{5}{c}{REGIONS}	
	1	2	3	4	5	U.S.
Infective & Parasitic Diseases	0.9	0.8	0.8	1.0	1.1	0.76
Malignant Neoplasms	19.2	19.1	19.6	19.9	20.6	18.4
Ischemic Heart Disease	28.0	28.9	28.1	27.2	27.4	25.0
Other Cardiovascular Disease	21.1	21.1	21.1	22.1	21.6	18.7
Influenza & Pneumonia	2.5	2.8	2.9	2.9	2.9	2.4
Bronchitis, Emphysema Asthma	3.0	3.8	3.1	2.6	3.0	2.5
Cirrhosis of Liver	0.8	1.0	1.5	1.0	1.6	1.4
Motor Vehicle Accidents	3.9	3.4	3.0	3.1	2.7	2.4
Other External Causes	6.5	6.5	6.0	5.6	5.4	4.7
Deaths from Other Causes	13.0	12.6	13.8	14.6	13.7	11.7
Total Deaths	8,806	15,366	15,028	6,851	14,196	
Region Size (Counties)	68	51	26	5	6	

Dominant Churches. In any overall regional analysis, religion is a strong element of cultural diversity. The map, Denominational Regions Based on Dominant Churches as a Percent of Total Churches, shows five regions with a general pattern of change from south to north (Figure 5). In this analysis any denomination having more than two percent of the total churches in the Southern Highlands was included.

Region 1 with 80 counties is by far the largest and most dominated by one denomination (Table 5). Southern Baptist Churches account for slightly more than 50 percent of all churches and United Methodist is the only other denomination with more than five percent of the total. This pattern is found in most counties in Georgia, South Carolina, North Carolina and Tennessee. Region 2 consists of 15 counties that reflect a slight Southern Baptist dominance but have important groups of United Methodist, Church of God (Cleveland) and Churches of Christ. Region 3 has 38 counties where the

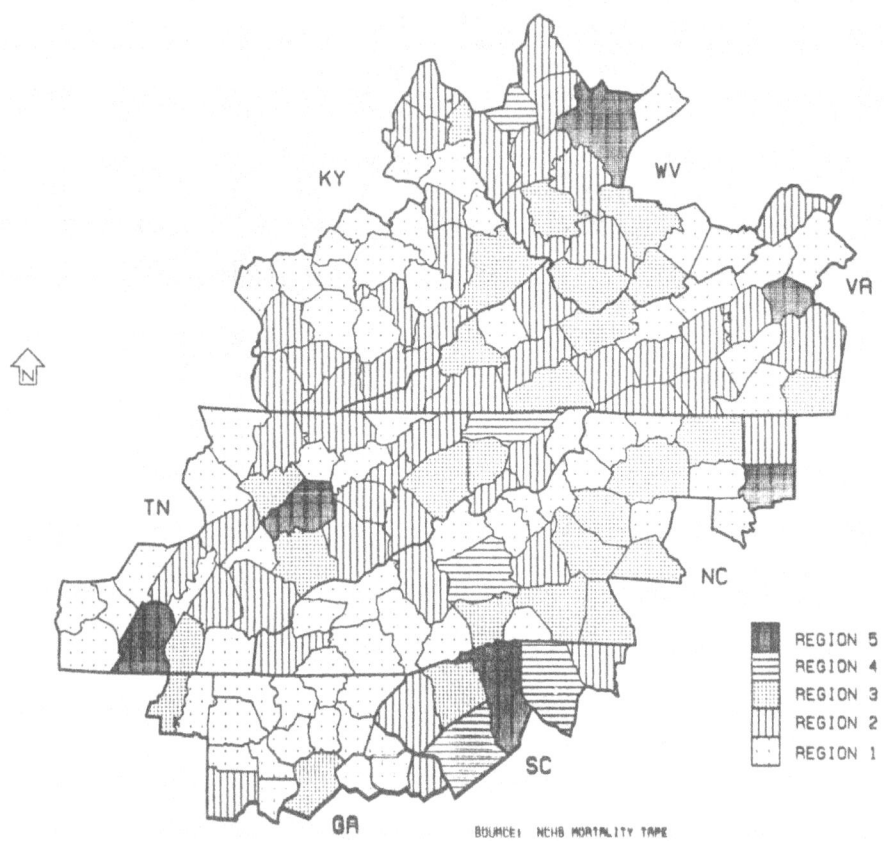

FIGURE 4.

Southern Baptist dominance has been replaced by United Methodist. This region also has the largest group of Presbyterian Churches in the U.S. Region 3 appears to be transitional between the southern and northern counties. Region 4 is made up of 12 counties with a central and northwesterly orientation. This region is dominated by Southern Baptist Churches but has the largest number of Christian Churches and Churches of Christ. United Methodist and Churches of Christ are also important. Region 5 is the smallest with only 11 counties. In this region the Southern Baptist influence has almost disappeared and United Methodist and American Baptist in the USA

TABLE 4
TOTAL DEATHS BY CAUSE
PER REGION - 1980

Cause	REGIONS				
	1	2	3	4	5
Infective & Parasitic Diseases	81.6	127.5	122.1	68.0	157.1
Malignant Neoplasms	1693.2	2927.4	2943.2	1362.0	2928.0
Ischemic Heart Disease	2468.4	4447.2	4225.0	1864.0	3892.2
Other Cardiovascular Disease	1856.4	3243.6	3172.0	1514.0	3067.2
Infleunza & Pneumonia	224.4	433.5	436.8	198.0	406.2
Bronchitis, Emphysema, Asthma	265.2	675.2	473.2	180.0	430.2
Cirrhosis of Liver	74.8	153.0	221.0	67.0	228.0
Motor Vehicle Accidents	340.0	520.2	449.0	221.0	385.8
Other Eternal Causes	571.2	999.6	904.8	387.0	760.2
Deaths from Other Causes	1149.2	1938.0	2080.0	1000.0	1941.0
Total Deaths	8,806	15,366	15,028	6,851	14,196
Region Size (Counties)	68	51	26	5	6

are dominant. Churches of Christ, Presbyterian Church in the U.S. and Church of God (Cleveland) are also important.

Multifactor Regions

Multiple factor regions can be developed by using various combinations of similar or dissimilar data. The data used may measure many different attributes of an area or its people. It is through this procedure that geographers undertake a task not done holistically by other disciplines. In other words through regional analysis geographers are not just interested in the classification of regions but attempt to understand the region as a whole.

The map, Multifactor Regions Based on 18 Socioeconomic Variables, gives an understanding of the spatial interaction of socioeconomic data by regions within the Southern Highlands (Figure 6). Here we see a mosaic of

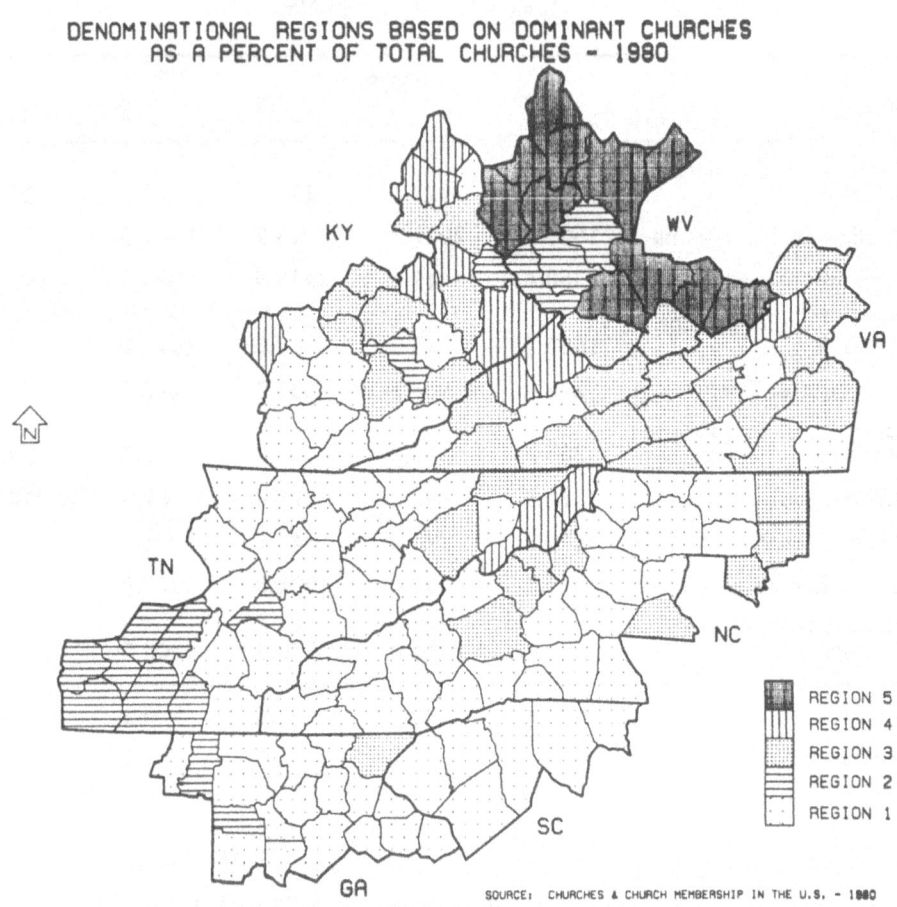

FIGURE 5.

regional characteristics, and many of our assumptions become more realistic when they are given this spatial dimension. We begin to see the answers to such questions as "What is the relationship between education and income?," "What is the relationship between birth rate and the ability of the population to support itself?," "Where are those areas most in need of public assistance?," "What are the basic needs of the people?," etc. (Table 6).

A close examination of the five regions presented here shows many relationships that are often considered singularly. It would seem that this ap-

TABLE 5
PERCENT OF CHURCHES BY DOMINANT DENOMINATION IN EACH REGION – 1980

DENOMINATION	REGIONS				
	1	2	3	4	5
Southern Baptist	51.0	26.7	22.8	29.1	2.3
United Methodist	17.9	16.5	27.0	14.8	26.5
Church of God (Cleveland)	4.9	15.7	3.8	4.4	5.2
Churches of Christ	3.0	13.4	3.6	10.6	7.3
Presbyterian Church in the U.S.	3.3	2.4	6.6	3.8	6.0
Christian Churches & Churches of Christ	2.1	1.1	3.7	19.7	2.3
American Baptist Churches in the USA	0.0	2.2	0.8	0.0	22.7
Other Churches	17.9	22.0	31.6	17.6	27.8
Region Size (Counties)	80	15	38	12	11

proach adds knowledge about the form and functions of areas and should be beneficial in both urban and regional planning. For example, Region 1 contains about 44 percent of the counties in the Southern Highlands—those that lie scattered along the central northeast-southwest axis of the overall region. Here in the Blue Ridge Mountains and in the Ridge and Valley section there is heavy dependence on manufacturing employment and little on agriculture or mining. There are comparatively low ratios of people on welfare, people living below the poverty level, and people living without adequate housing (reflected by inadequate plumbing). The population is aging and there is a high proportion of females in the labor force. For planning purposes it can be surmised that while local government officials will need to be concerned with economic development, some additional effort will need to be exerted toward revitalization of the farm economy. Although furnishing additional facilities for elementary education will probably not become a problem, continuing education for adults will need to be made more available as well as child care for the high percentage of female workers in the labor force.

Region 2, the least contiguous in the overall region, contains only about 10 percent of the counties in the Southern Highlands. Median home values are the highest among the five regions, yet there are still a number of homes

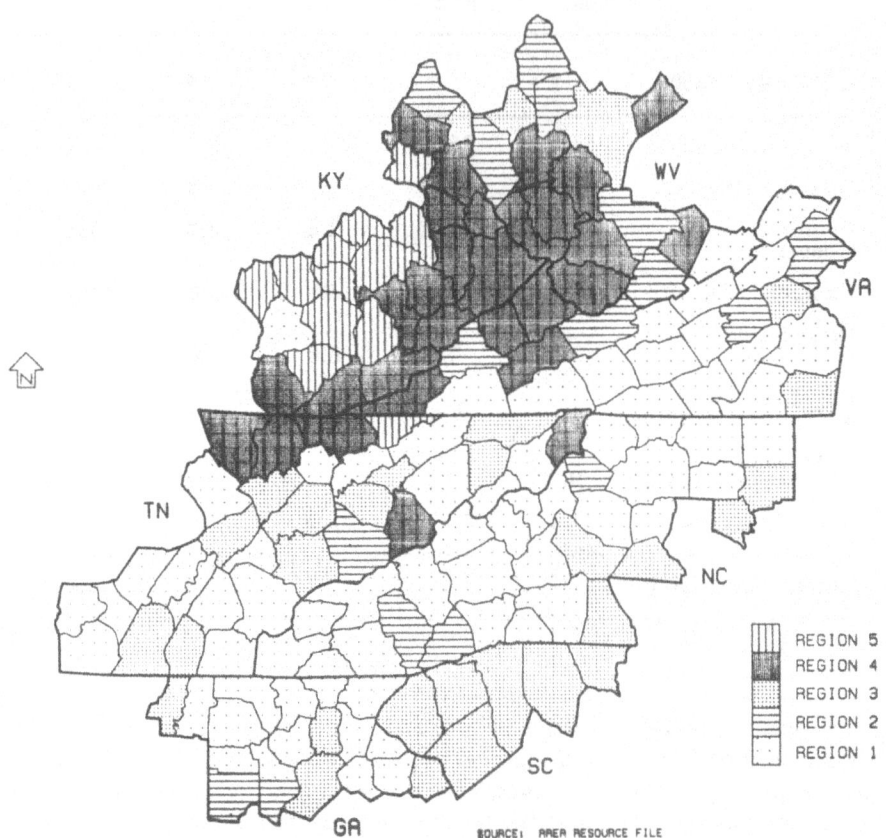

FIGURE 6.

without adequate plumbing; education levels are high and poverty levels lower than in three of the five regions. Because median ages are lower there may have to be more planning efforts in regard to the education of younger children.

Region 3, with 19 percent of the counties, portrays clearly the results of economic diversification. High percentages of the labor force are in manufacturing and services (with a large proportion of employed females) and a low percentage in agriculture. Implications here are that people in this region sustain higher levels of living than do those in the other four regions.

TABLE 6
AVERAGE VALUE BY REGIONS OF DATA USED IN
MULTIFACTOR REGIONALIZATION SCHEME

SIC CLASS	REGIONS				
	1	2	3	4	5
Percent Black Population	4.1	3.0	12.1	2.1	0.5
Percent of Families with Female Head	11.0	10.3	13.7	11.8	11.9
Birth Rate	12.9	14.3	14.1	16.6	17.4
Median Age	32.1	29.4	30.9	28.3	28.1
Infant Mortality Rate	13.0	13.0	12.1	12.1	11.2
Death Rate	9.0	7.9	8.7	9.2	8.6
Per Capita Income	6,549	7,114	8,381	6,425	4,732
Percent of Persons Below Poverty Level	15.6	14.0	12.3	23.1	37.0
Percent of Females Divorced	5.1	5.0	7.2	5.1	5.3
AFDC Recipients as a Percent of Total Population	1.8	2.6	2.7	5.6	9.0
Percent of Labor Force in Agriculture, Forestry, Fisheries and Mining	4.7	8.5	1.9	25.5	13.8
Percent of Labor Force in Manufacturing	36.8	17.0	31.9	9.8	10.7
Females, 16 Years and Older as a Percent of the Labor Force	41.7	37.1	45.3	32.5	28.1
Unemployment Rate, 16 Years and Older	6.7	7.5	6.1	11.0	11.9
White Collar Workers, 16 Years and Older, as a Percent of the Labor Force	32.7	40.6	47.2	31.5	24.7
Median School Years Completed, 25 Years and Older	10.4	11.8	11.5	9.4	7.4
Median Home Value	29,997	39,794	35,656	26,151	20,558
Percent of Housing Units Without Plumbing	6.2	5.1	2.1	11.6	24.3
Region Size (Counties)	69	16	30	29	12

Region 4, with another 19 percent of the counties of the Southern Highlands (mostly in the "coal counties" of Kentucky, Virginia, and West Virginia), depicts the results of mining as a large employer of people, without concurrent emphasis on manufacturing and services employment. Also, home values are low (as in home quality), there is low utilization of females in the labor force and unemployment is high. In this region planners and other officials will need to focus their efforts on greater economic diversification, improvement of education, better delivery of social services, and the like.

The 12 counties of Region 5, composing only 8 percent of 156 counties of the overall region, and bordering on Region 4, is the Southern Highlands real "disaster area." With one exception these counties are located on the Appalachian Plateau in Kentucky; home values, home quality, per capita income, and education are the lowest of the five regions. In addition, birth rates are high as are rates of unemployment, persons living below the poverty level and welfare recipients. It is obvious that social planning and economic development planning will have to be based on some new concepts if the levels of living in this sub-region are to be brought into line with those of even the next poorest area.

Summary And Conclusions

The whole idea of regionalization has to do with people's perceptions of place. In the broadest sense it is a frame of reference as to what a place or area is like. Once the character has been determined, the concept can be used in its simplest terms to demonstrate how seemingly unrelated elements of data can be used to portray the existence of and to analyze composite patterns in an area as complex as the Southern Highlands. Different regions exhibited in this paper have been derived by combining various qualities, attributes and/or properties in order to gain a better understanding as to how some areas within a larger region can be different from other areas within that same region.

The use of this regionalization technique can hopefully lead to a greater understanding of the region and its people as regional differences can be delimited and then linked to differences in local governmental leadership styles. Hopefully, planning and decision-making that are based on regional understandings will be superior to that accomplished only by intuition.

www.ingramcontent.com/pod-product-compliance
Lightning Source LLC
Chambersburg PA
CBHW070920160426
43193CB00011B/1536